PHYSICAL EDUCATION
IN THE PRIMARY SCHOOL

The exhilaration of height and flight

PHYSICAL EDUCATION
IN THE
PRIMARY SCHOOL

A. BILBROUGH

Diploma, Carnegie College of Physical Education
Senior Organiser of Physical Education, Lancashire County Council
Previously Organiser of Physical Education, Halifax

and

P. JONES

Diploma, Carnegie College of Physical Education
Area Organiser of Physical Education
Lancashire County Council

UNIVERSITY OF LONDON PRESS LTD

SBN 340 08987 3

First published 1963
Third edition: second impression 1968
Copyright © 1968 A. Bilbrough and P. Jones

University of London Press Ltd
St Paul's House, Warwick Lane, London EC4

Printed and bound in England by
Hazell Watson & Viney Ltd, Aylesbury, Bucks

Contents

5

practices—teaching method—summary of jumping practices—summary of the technique of jumping. Footwork: activities for the feet and ankles—teaching method—recreative foot activities

List of Plates

Preface to the Third Edition

OUR main object in writing this book is to set down, as clearly and as simply as we can, our interpretation of some of the salient features of recent developments in Physical Education in the Primary School. Without going very deeply into the theories and philosophies involved, we aim to give some positive and practical guidance regarding the content and method of the Primary School P.E. lesson. From our own experiences we suggest ways of applying principles which are based on common sense and sound reason, and illustrate our suggestions by reference to work being done with great success in all types of Primary Schools.

We realise the many problems which Primary School teachers face when Physical Education is only one of the many subjects they have to teach and lack of time prevents them from giving it the detailed and careful study which is expected of the specialist. Primarily, therefore, this book has been written for 'class teachers' and students, many of whom have requested help with interpreting the new approach to P.E. On the other hand, successful work at Secondary level depends largely upon the work done in the Primary School, so we hope that it will also be of value to specialist teachers in Secondary Schools.

This edition, thoroughly revised, includes a substantial amount of new material, especially in the chapters on Jumping and Landing, Balance, Group Work, the use of Large Apparatus, Schemes of Work and Lesson Preparation. Nine additional diagrams further illustrate the text and there are twenty-five new photographs.

Our sincere thanks are due to the many head teachers, staff and children for their help and co-operation, to Mr. K. Oldham of Nelson and Mr. A. I. Oldham of Manchester for the photographs and to Mr. R. P. Hartley of Brierfield for providing material for the diagrams.

9

CHAPTER I

Introduction

The post-war period has seen considerable progress in Physical Education, particularly in the development of trends of thought which were finding expression in some schools even before 1939. This has been particularly true in the field of Primary School Physical Education, where the changes can be regarded as revolutionary. Experimental work of various kinds has provided teachers and children with stimulating and invigorating experiences and its success is reflected in the extremely enthusiastic attitude of both teachers and children.

Aims of Physical Education in the Primary School

The general aims of Physical Education do not change fundamentally over the years. The foremost aim is the education of the 'whole' child—a phrase which is very familiar to all those interested in education. It implies that due attention is being given to the maximum development of each individual child, physically, mentally, morally and socially, in the preparation for life and for living. To give material help to each child during the vital growing period of school life, the physical education scheme must concern itself with efforts 'to secure and maintain high standards of bodily health', with the correction of physical defects and with the development of physique and vigour.

These involve the development of the physical ability of each child in as wide a variety of recreational, athletic and gymnastic activities as possible, so that the child not only learns to appreciate the sheer joy of physical fitness and well-being, but acquires a desire for participation in healthy physical activity. In more specific terms we would summarise the aims of the class teacher in Physical Education as follows:

1 To contribute to the physical development of each child.
2 To increase the physical skill of each child, developing versatility, adaptability and the ability to cope with various tasks and situations.
3 To enable each child, through physical activity, to experience a sense of achievement as frequently as possible.
4 To help children to experience the enjoyment associated with well-planned, stimulating and purposeful lessons.
5 To help children to learn how to co-operate with each other and to work successfully as members of a group.
6 To exercise the natural learning processes of enquiry and discovery through creative and imaginative physical activity.
7 To develop physical and mental co-ordination, self-control and confidence.
8 To provide opportunities for a wide experience in all types of movements and activities, both with and without apparatus, and for using all kinds of apparatus in as many different ways as possible.

Why have we summarised our aims in this way? Teachers need some firm principles upon which to assess the value or otherwise of their work, and it is necessary, periodically, to ask whether in fact the type of work being done is contributing positively to the development of the natural learning processes. We should ask ourselves:

Do the children have opportunities to be creative?
Do the children have opportunities to practise freely?
Do the children have opportunities to exercise choice?
Are there signs of improving physical ability and understanding?
Is the work enjoyable as well as beneficial?
Do all the children have an opportunity to enjoy a sense of achievement?

Our results must be measured in the light of our aims. What means do we employ to ensure that these aims are achieved? Are these means very different from those employed by Primary School teachers in the past?

The scheme of Physical Education is based on the child as an individual and upon the needs, the developing physique, the physical ability and the personality of each child. Movement is as individual as the individual child and attempts to force all children to conform exactly to a common pattern all the time are educationally unsound. The aim of the teacher must be to assist each child to attain the maximum development possible for that child. This can be done in many different ways, but whatever the approach or method used, all teachers will agree that they are concerned with the same problems, and that they are aiming to develop to the full the varying physical resources of each individual, so that he or she will be able to use them effectively in all physical situations, and in the many aspects of Physical Education.

The emphasis on the individual shows itself in a variety of ways. There is a greater readiness to allow scope for personal variations and interpretations of the same activity, even when the activity is either teacher-guided or even teacher-directed. Although the children may all be practising the same movement, the teacher is willing to recognise that there might be as many different ways of performing that movement as there are children in the class. In addition, each child will, in time, discover that he is capable of performing that movement in many different ways. Opportunity for individual practice has become a feature of the Physical Education lesson, which has assumed an air of informality far removed from the militarised 'drill' from which it has developed. The accent is on activity and movement of a purposeful character. The teacher adopts a much more conversational manner, coaching, encouraging, stimulating, suggesting and making greater use of observation by the children to help them to appreciate and improve their own ability and to understand the purpose of their efforts. Perhaps even more revolutionary is the frequent opportunity provided for the children to choose their own activity and to build on what they have done by further experiment and invention. By these modifications of traditional work it has become possible for individual children to make progress at their own rate. As this principle is generally accepted, no child feels inadequate or insecure because of a lack of ability or confidence.

How does the teacher ensure that these individual needs are

met? How does he succeed in regarding the class no longer as a class unit but as a number of individuals developing daily in physique, ability and personality? This is achieved in many ways, for example:

(a) By permitting the children to practise freely, in their own time, while the teacher coaches and guides an individual, a group, or the whole class.

(b) By allowing opportunities for a choice of activity by each child, either freely or within limits set by the teacher, the apparatus, or the space available.

(c) By appreciating the fact that progress in physical ability varies with each child, and by allowing each child to make such progress at his or her own rate.

(d) By realising that, although children may vary in ability, each is capable of an individual maximum effort and by encouraging each child to make that effort.

Where does Physical Education fit into the Primary School scheme? Any aspect of education which gives a child a sense of achievement is valuable and Physical Education in its modern conception can give this to most children. For some children, in fact, it provides the opportunity to experience a sense of achievement which otherwise they might never enjoy. In addition, the achievement experienced through successful participation in physical activity often provides the incentive which enables a child to overcome difficulties met in other subjects. If the teacher really believes this, then Physical Education will be given an equal place with other, more academic, subjects in the curriculum.

Games of all kinds, cricket, football, netball, rounders, stool-ball, minor games and games practices, together with swimming, simple athletics practices and dancing, will all have their place in the Primary School Physical Education scheme, for all play their part in achieving the ultimate aim. Together with the Gymnastics lesson, these form the school's Physical Education programme.

Comments on some aspects of modern developments

The most revolutionary change that has taken place in recent years has been in the teaching method employed in the P.E. lesson. Although the content of the lesson has undergone a change and adult-imposed artificial exercises have been discarded in favour of natural movements and activities, it is the actual presentation of the work that has been most affected by modern trends of thought. These changes include:

(*a*) An analysis and appreciation of movement much broader than the purely anatomical analysis previously used.

(*b*) A recognition of the fact that selection of exercises on a purely chronological basis is unreliable and that the teaching method used must allow for variation in physique and physical ability.

(*c*) A greater recognition of the value of 'group' work in every lesson, a feature which was often neglected because of the insistence on a full 'table' of exercises being completed in Part I of the lesson.

(*d*) A recognition of the fact that the physical ability of children in the Primary School has been grossly underestimated.

(*e*) The need for less formality, which has been a feature of developments made since the turn of the century.

(*f*) A discontinuation of the use of 'four straight lines' and similar class formations in favour of a free use of floor space.

(*g*) The discarding of formal 'drill' commands in favour of the more natural teaching manner of the classroom.

(*h*) Opportunities for children to practise on their own, in their own time, as opposed to performing class-controlled exercises in unison.

(*i*) Opportunities for a free choice of activity by each individual child rather than teacher-directed class exercises.

(*j*) Opportunities for experimentation, exploration and discovery.

(*k*) Opportunities for children to use their imagination and creative skill.

(*l*) Opportunities for partner and group co-operation in addition to work of a purely individual nature.

ay of storing hoops
ual mats—a solution in restricted space
rolley, converted from an old desk
oring canes

[17

(*m*) The increased use of demonstration and observation, which enables children to understand more clearly what they do and how they do it.
(*n*) The provision of a greater variety of small apparatus which makes the work more purposeful and objective, particularly with younger children.
(*o*) The introduction of large equipment to provide opportunities for activities such as hanging, climbing, jumping, balancing.

The teacher

Although Physical Education is based on the importance of the child as an individual, we must also recognise that teachers are individuals and that the method used by each teacher is entirely a personal matter depending upon his own personality, his ability and his belief in the principles associated with modern Physical Education. How far he is willing to adopt modern methods will vary with each individual teacher.

No one person can evolve a perfect system of teaching Physical Education, except possibly for himself, but there are certain basic principles which are fundamental to success and which all teachers should understand and apply. Some teachers have accepted everything that is new because it is new, while others have rejected everything new for the same reason. Wise teachers will examine new ideas, try them out, and sift the good from the bad.

Mr. E. Major, former Staff Inspector of Physical Education, once said: 'I am sure that the future development of Physical Education lies in the ability of the teacher to experiment courageously, to clarify his principles, to keep a balanced view of what he hopes to achieve, and to select the material and method of presentation in a way that will best meet these ends.'

The main problems facing a teacher of any subject are: organisation and preparation; lesson content and material, and methods of presentation; implementation—including methods of development; and for real success none of these should be neglected. It is most important, however, to realise that we are teachers of children as well as teachers of a subject, and that P.E., if well taught, will have a profound and beneficial effect upon the 'whole' child.

15

CHAPTER 2

Apparatus

Types

The apparatus used in Primary Schools is of two main types: *small apparatus*, such as (*a*) small balls, hoops, wooden blocks, etc., and (*b*) games equipment; and *large apparatus*, which is either (*a*) portable, such as climbing frames, benches, mats, etc., or (*b*) fixed, such as climbing ropes, parallel ropes, scrambling nets, etc.

Scale of supply

The following scale of apparatus is suggested as sufficient to meet the needs of a Primary School. Where an item of small apparatus is recommended for each child, e.g. a small ball or an individual rubber mat, the actual number required should be equivalent to the number of children in the largest class. A school thus acquires a stock of apparatus which is sufficient for the largest class and available for use by each class during its Physical Education lesson.

SMALL APPARATUS

(*a*) 1 small ball ($2\frac{1}{2}$ in.–$2\frac{3}{4}$ in.) per child.
1 individual rubber mat (36 in. × 18 in.) per child.
1 skipping rope per child (Infants, 7 ft–8 ft; Juniors, 8 ft–9 ft).
1 wooden block (Infants, 10 in. × $2\frac{1}{2}$ in. × $2\frac{1}{2}$ in.; Juniors, 12 in. × 3 in. × 3 in.) per child.
1 hoop (varying sizes, 18 in., 24 in., 30 in., 36 in.) per child.
1 cane (4 ft) between two children.
1 playbat between two children.
1 plastic gamester ball between two children.
1 dozen rubber quoits.

16

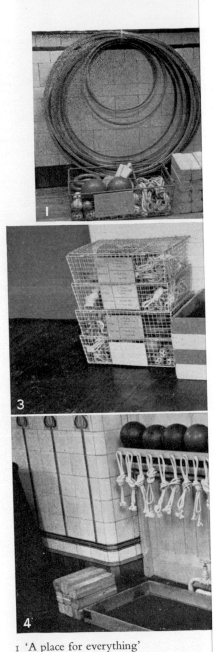

1 'A place for everything'
2 The 'orange-box' store
3 Nesting containers for small apparatus
4 'Everything in its place'—another solut
5 An effective v
6 Storing indivi
7 An apparatus
8 One way of s

16]

1 dozen beanbags (4 in. × 4 in., or 4 in. × 6 in.); for Infants, one beanbag per child.

4 canes (6 ft or 7 ft).

8 large rubber or plastic balls (5 in.–7½ in.).

2 long ropes (15 ft–21 ft).

4 to 8 extending skittles (Infants, 12 in.–20 in.; Juniors, 20 in.–36 in.).

6 vaulting poles (5 ft) with rubber ferrules (Juniors only).

1 set jumping stands (Junior size).

(*b*) *Games equipment*

In addition to the small apparatus, the following games equipment should be available:

Shinty or Hockey sticks and balls.

Footballs (size 3).

Netballs (size 4).

Cricket equipment.

Rounders bats, sticks, balls and bases.

Stool-ball equipment.

Batinton, Padder-tennis equipment, etc.

The number of items purchased should be sufficient to enable games and practices to be carried out in pairs or small groups.

LARGE APPARATUS

(*a*) *Portable*

4 balancing benches (9 ft for Infants, or 11 ft for Juniors).

8 or more rubber landing mats (4 ft × 3 ft or 5 ft × 4 ft).

1 or more climbing units in wood or tubular steel.

1 vaulting box (Junior size).

2 or more sets of 'jumping' boxes (see Plate 25).

2 wooden trestles (2 ft–2 ft 6 in. high) (see Plate 21).

(*b*) *Fixed*

Two or three pieces of fixed equipment for such activities as heaving, climbing or hanging, selected from the wide range now available, e.g rope and wood window ladders, parallel ropes, climbing ropes, scrambling nets, etc.

The provision of this type of equipment for Primary School children is a welcome development of recent years (see p. 139). The opportunity to climb and heave on large apparatus was previously provided in secondary schools only, but the physical development which has resulted amongst Primary School children, to whom these facilities have been extended, has fully justified the change. Moreover, the thrill which young children experience when working or 'playing' on this equipment is further justification for its provision. In addition, there is great opportunity for the exercise of initiative, enterprise and courage.

In schools of three streams or more, it is usually necessary to have a duplicate set of small equipment, because two classes often have their P.E. lessons at the same time. It is not suggested that such schools will need a duplicate set of large apparatus, especially of the fixed type, though it will be necessary to arrange for all the children to have regular opportunities to use it. Some duplication of large portable apparatus might be considered advisable.

Priorities

When making initial purchases of small apparatus and where financial resources are limited, it is recommended that the apparatus be purchased in the following order of priority:

(a) Small balls.
(b) Individual rubber mats.
(c) Skipping ropes.
(d) Large rubber or plastic balls.
(e) Playbats and gamester balls.
(f) Wooden blocks and canes.
(g) Hoops, etc.

When making initial purchases of large apparatus the following order of priority is recommended:

(a) An item of climbing apparatus.
(b) Four rubber landing mats.
(c) Two benches (for jumping, balancing, etc.).
(d) A second piece of climbing apparatus.

(e) A vaulting box (Junior size) and/or a set of jumping boxes.

(f) Two or more rubber landing mats.

(g) One or two wooden trestles.

(h) A third piece of climbing apparatus.

(i) Other items of jumping apparatus—e.g. boxes, benches, etc.

Organisation and use of small apparatus

One of the features of modern Primary School Physical Education is the greater use of small apparatus (see Chapter 9). In order that the pace and vigour of the lesson may be maintained, it is essential that thought be given to the best and quickest way of providing each child or group with apparatus. In some schools the small apparatus can be left permanently in the hall, but in others it is necessary to store it in some other convenient place. It is essential in such schools to devise a scheme which ensures that the apparatus is taken out and put away as quickly, effectively and efficiently as possible. It is usually possible to do this at the beginning and end of the day by means of a monitorial system, so that the apparatus is in place ready for each class to use. Unnecessary moving of apparatus between lessons should be avoided if at all possible.

Dispersal

Small apparatus should be dispersed in order to save time and avoid crowding and jostling when it is being collected or returned. Methods will vary from school to school, but in most cases it will be found better to disperse the apparatus into at least four groups, and, depending upon the type of containers used for this purpose

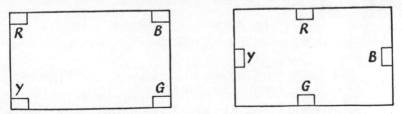

R. B, G, Y – Red, blue, green, yellow apparatus corners or places

FIG. 1

and the amount of space available, this is best done by placing the apparatus near the corners of the hall or playground, and preferably against the wall (as suggested in Fig. 1).

The children should be divided into the appropriate number of groups and trained to collect their items of apparatus from the same place, the same basket, the same pile of mats, etc., every time they use them. Fig. 2 shows, in diagrammatic form, a suitable arrangement of the apparatus in a group or team corner.

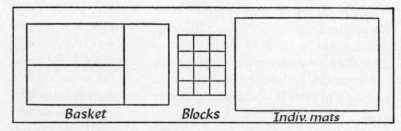

Basket   Blocks   Indiv. mats

FIG. 2

The basket contains the group's small apparatus, such as balls, ropes, beanbags, playbats, quoits, etc., and there should be sufficient apparatus in the corner to meet the requirements of each child in the group. A coloured label with a list of contents fixed to the basket is a great help, and the painting of wooden blocks, together with coloured markings on the small balls, mats, ropes, etc., makes checking of apparatus a much simpler task. It has also been found helpful to have lines or marks painted on the floor to indicate the permanent position of the various items. A place for everything and everything in its place should be the rule, and the rule should be rigidly kept.

Time is well spent in training the children in the drills of collecting, carrying and returning apparatus. This is essential.

E.g. (a) Individual mats should be carried with both hands.
(b) Mats should be returned in pairs, clean sides together.
(c) Apparatus should be placed, not thrown, in the appropriate compartment of the basket.
(d) Skipping ropes should be knotted.

Suggestions for using individual rubber mats

1 Mark one side with coloured paint, so that the same side of the mat always goes to the floor.

2 Teach the children to put the mats away in pairs with the clean sides together, thus preserving the cleanliness of one side as much as possible. The children should do this with partners from their own groups.

3 Teach the correct method of carrying the mats—both hands holding the long side of the mat.

4 Ensure that the mats are dispersed at the beginning of the lesson and returned neatly to their original places.

5 Train the children to collect their mats in an orderly manner, always taking the top mat.

6 The mats should be placed, not thrown, on the floor.

7 Each mat should be placed on the floor in such a way that there is as much space around it as possible.

8 When the children are wearing plimsolls, they should be encouraged to keep their feet off the mats.

9 For many reasons, it is an advantage to have all the mats facing in the same direction, especially for demonstration purposes, for observation by the teacher, and as a safety measure when practising activities on the hands, etc.

Fig. 3 illustrates an effective way of spacing the mats on the floor, but the children do this themselves.

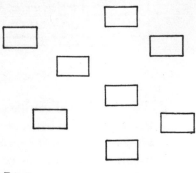

FIG. 3

Suggestions for the use of nesting baskets for small P.E. apparatus

Wire baskets which nest on each other in sets of four (see Plate 3) have proved to be one satisfactory solution to the storage problem, for the following reasons:

1 They can be fastened together by means of a separate lid and locking bar, and thus provide safe storage facilities.
2 They facilitate the dispersal of small equipment and thus assist in the organisation, discipline and conduct of the lesson.
3 They can be taken outside without much difficulty or inconvenience.
4 If carefully used, they prolong the life of the equipment stored in them.

Preparation and marking of baskets

1 *Coloured labels* (size 9 in. × 6 in. approximately).
   (*a*) Each basket can be labelled with a specific colour—each label indicating the contents of the basket and the disposition of the apparatus within it, as, for example, in Fig. 4.

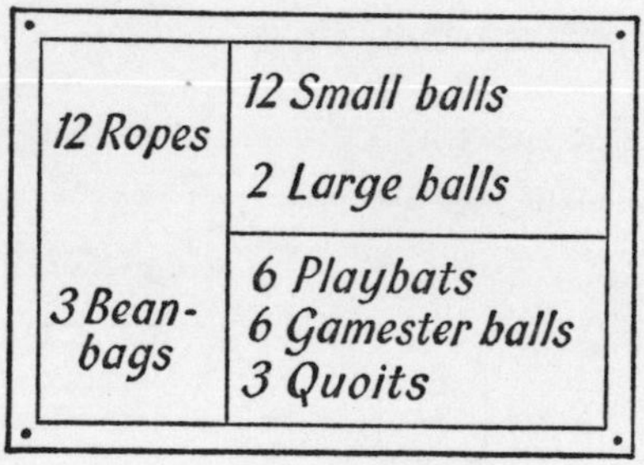

12 Ropes	12 Small balls
	2 Large balls
3 Bean-bags	6 Playbats
	6 Gamester balls
	3 Quoits

FIG. 4

Although coloured cardboard will fulfil this purpose temporarily, it is advisable, as a more permanent measure, to mount the cardboard on hardboard or plywood. Transparent celluloid or perspex will provide additional protection against normal wear and tear (Fig. 5).

(*b*) At first, particularly with younger children, it will be better for each compartment to be labelled with its contents, despite the fact that these are also indicated on the main basket label.

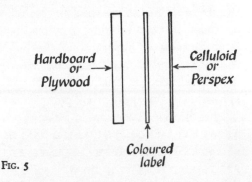

Hardboard or Plywood →

← Celluloid or Perspex

↑ Coloured label

FIG. 5

2 *Contents*. As far as possible each basket should hold the same amount of apparatus and the following arrangement is suggested (based on a class of 40–48 children):

Compartment No. 1—10–12 ropes; 3–6 beanbags.
Compartment No. 2—10–12 small balls; 2 large balls.
Compartment No. 3—5–6 playbats; 5–6 stocking balls or gamester balls; 3 quoits.

3 *Marking of apparatus*. Schools might consider marking the handles of playbats, the ends of ropes and balls (by painting on a coloured spot) with an appropriate colour—e.g. red, green, yellow or blue. The advantage of this marking is that, in the event of apparatus from any basket being lost, it can be traced to the children using that basket. It also serves to remind children of the basket to which their apparatus should be returned.

4 *Position of baskets*. Time will be saved in the lesson if each basket, when in use, has a permanent position in the school hall or playground. A common policy for all teachers in the school will avoid confusion and unnecessary moving of baskets from lesson to lesson.

23

Training of the children

If the best use is to be made of the baskets, it is essential that the children should receive adequate training. Respect for the apparatus is an important part of the social training of children; they should be trained to use the same basket each time small apparatus is needed and this should guarantee that each basket contains the same amount of apparatus at the beginning and at the end of the lesson. Unless this is done the main purpose and value of the baskets will be lost. Furthermore, the children should replace the apparatus in the appropriate compartment.

The following rules should be observed: (a) ALWAYS COLLECT APPARATUS FROM THE SAME BASKET; and (b) REPLACE APPARATUS IN THE RIGHT BASKET AND IN THE RIGHT COMPARTMENT. Time will be well spent in teaching children these drills. If the system is to be successful it is necessary that each class and each teacher should see that the baskets are left in readiness for the next.

At the end of the lesson the teacher should arrange for children to check the contents and disposition of the apparatus in each basket. Missing equipment should be traced immediately. Where necessary, the baskets should be locked at the end of each session, day or week. The children can do this. Unless each basket is locked inside the one below it, by means of the protruding lugs, they will come apart easily.

The success of a lesson largely depends on the efficient organisation of the apparatus and, obvious though these points may seem, they are essential to success.

Storage of small apparatus

The storage of small apparatus is a problem in most schools. The nesting containers already referred to in this chapter have provided in many schools a suitable storage place. The four containers nest on top of each other and, fastened by the locking device, are put away in a corner of the hall or classroom until apparatus is needed again. One of the main advantages of these nesting containers is that they solve two problems at the same

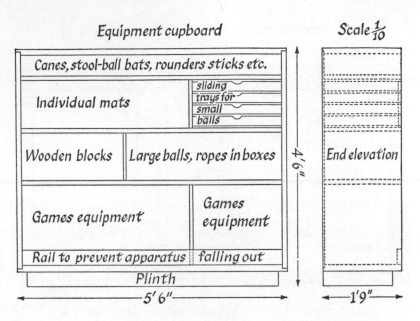

Equipment cupboard   Scale $\frac{1}{10}$

Canes, stool-ball bats, rounders sticks etc.

Individual mats — sliding trays for small balls

Wooden blocks | Large balls, ropes in boxes | End elevation

Games equipment | Games equipment

Rail to prevent apparatus | falling out

Plinth

4' 6"

5' 6"

1' 9"

Fig. 6

time, the problem of satisfactory dispersal and the problem of suitable storage.

Some schools do not find it necessary to lock their apparatus away and have provided apparatus boxes or trays which are stored permanently in the hall where they are used. Some schools have had special equipment cupboards made; other schools put their containers away and have had special cupboards made for this purpose. Plates 1–8 and Fig. 6 illustrate how several schools have solved their storage problems.

The individual rubber mats create an additional problem where storage is not easy and the following suggestions are put forward:

1 A portable trolley (see Plate 6).
2 A portable trolley in sets of 4 for mats and other small apparatus (see Plate 7 and Fig. 7).
3 Portable mat trays (see Plate 3).
4 Special cupboards which hold mats and other small apparatus (see Fig. 6).

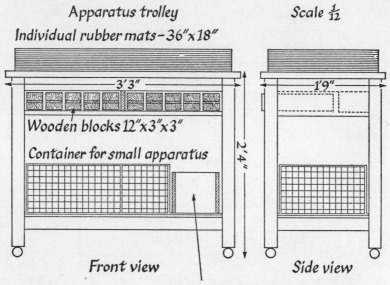

Apparatus trolley   Scale $\frac{1}{12}$

Individual rubber mats – 36″ x 18″

3′3″

Wooden blocks 12″x3″x3″

Container for small apparatus

2′4″

1′9″

Front view   Side view

Wooden box for large balls etc.

Fig. 7

Additional suggestions for the storage of small apparatus

1 Nesting containers (usually four) to hold sufficient small balls, large balls, gamester or stocking balls, playbats, rubber quoits, beanbags and skipping ropes for the whole class.

2 Small balls—biscuit tins, fruit baskets, cake trays, etc.

3 Large balls—fruit baskets, waste-paper baskets or large plastic bowls.

    —resting on rubber quoits on suitable window ledges.

4 Individual mats—trays of the box type (inside measurements 39 in. $\times$ 21 in. $\times$ 3½ in.) (see Plate 3).

    —trays of the 'duckboard' type (39 in. $\times$ 21 in.).

    —hardboard trays (39 in. $\times$ 21 in.).

    —mat trolley, particularly valuable where it is necessary to store the mats away from the hall.

5 Hoops—hoop stand (see Plate 5).

    —suspended on brackets fixed to the wall (see Plate 1).

6 Canes—small drain pipe.
      —horizontally on two angle brackets on the wall.
      —vertically held by brackets on the wall (see Plate 8).
      —suspended from small hooks on a wall or rail (see
        Plate 4).
7 Ropes—small baskets.
      —suspended from small hooks on a wall or rail (see
        Plate 4).
8 Playbats—suspended from small hooks by a loop of string
        through the handles.
9 Wooden blocks—wooden boxes with appropriate handles.

A most effective improvised container can be made by using orange boxes as shown in Plate 2. Four of these boxes, each painted in a different colour, are placed in the four corners of the room or playground. Each will hold the following:

(a) On the top—a tray or 'tidy box' containing 12 small balls standing on a similar box holding 6 or more beanbags and 6 gamester balls.

(b) On the middle shelf—12 wooden blocks and 6 playbats.

(c) On the bottom—6 large balls.

(d) On the sides—knotted ropes on hooks, rubber quoits on a rope loop.

Boxes can be strengthened by fastening strips of wood across the top, both front and back, and this also helps to hold the 'tidy boxes' in place. In the same way, a strip of wood fastened inside the box on the front edge of the bottom shelf helps to strengthen the box and prevents balls falling out.

Teachers and children share the responsibility for the efficient organisation of the use and care of the apparatus. Children quickly realise what is expected of them, and will respond well if they know that their efforts are appreciated. Teachers must always insist on proper attention being given to the training of the children in the use and care of the apparatus. Good team work by all teachers using the apparatus is essential and very rewarding.

CHAPTER 3

Teaching Method

General principles

In the Physical Education lesson, both the selection of suitable material and also the method of its presentation are of the greatest importance and the whole purpose of recent changes is lost if the traditional command–response method of instruction alone is used. The first essential for the teacher of Physical Education is to adopt a much more natural and conversational manner than was used previously, and to speak to the children in the same way as in any other lesson. Formal 'drill' commands should be discarded in favour of a more informal approach, using a quiet speaking voice as in the classroom. To make this effective, all the children should be able to hear clearly what the teacher is saying, so they must be expected to work quietly. When introducing this informal and conversational method to children who have previously been used to the more formal approach, it will be found that there is a tendency for the class to be noisy, especially in the early stages. The teacher should never try to compete with the class in making noise—a quiet teacher produces a quiet class, and children soon learn to work quietly.

Good discipline is essential, but the teacher's aim should be self-discipline by the child, obtained through concentration, interest and enthusiasm, rather than discipline imposed by the teacher. Freedom must not become chaos.

Methods of presentation

For convenience and clarity we have analysed methods of presentation under three main headings:

1 the Direct Method;
2 the Indirect Method;
3 the Limitation Method.

The method of presentation employed is determined by the amount of choice allowed to the children. When there is 100 per cent limitation and the choice of activity or movement is entirely that of the teacher, the teaching method employed is known as the Direct Method. When the choice of activity is left entirely to the children, and the only limitation imposed upon them is that of the apparatus being used, then the teaching method employed is known as the Indirect Method.

When the choice of activity or movement is limited by some factor other than that of the apparatus, then the teaching method employed is known as the Limitation Method. This in effect is a combination or blending of the Direct and Indirect Methods.

Figure 8 on the next page has been devised to illustrate the ways in which the work can be presented.

From this diagram it will be seen that there are seven basic variations of the method form and an example of each method is given below:

1 Practise 'Bunny Jumps'.
2 Each take a skipping rope and practise skipping on the spot with both feet together.
3 Practise any movement or activity you wish without apparatus.
4 Get a small mat each and practise freely.
5 Get any piece of small apparatus and practise any activity of your own choice.
6 Moving anywhere in the hall, practise any kind of jumping and landing movement.
7 Each take a small ball and practise any activity with the ball in the air.

It will be seen that even when one type of apparatus is used, any of the three methods can be equally effective. For example, using a rubber mat for each child, the teacher might say:

(a) Practise a 'Bunny Jump' across your mat. (Direct)
or (b) Practise freely on your mat. (Indirect)

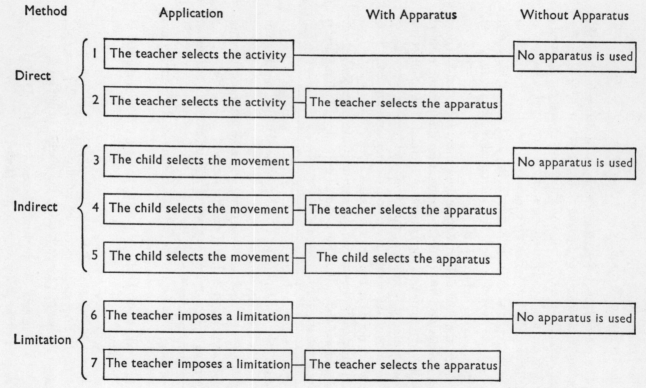

Method	Application	With Apparatus	Without Apparatus
Direct	1 The teacher selects the activity		No apparatus is used
	2 The teacher selects the activity	The teacher selects the apparatus	
Indirect	3 The child selects the movement		No apparatus is used
	4 The child selects the movement	The teacher selects the apparatus	
	5 The child selects the movement	The child selects the apparatus	
Limitation	6 The teacher imposes a limitation		No apparatus is used
	7 The teacher imposes a limitation	The teacher selects the apparatus	

FIG. 8

or (c) On your mat practise any kind of stretching and curling movement. (Limitation)

In just the same way these three methods of presentation are equally successful when no apparatus is being used. For example, the teacher might say:

(a) Practise cartwheels. (Direct)
or (b) Practise any movement or activity without apparatus. (Indirect)
or (c) Practise any movement where you take your weight on your hands. (Limitation)

There are many arguments (to be discussed later) for and against free and directed work, but experience has shown that a combination of all three methods, even in one lesson, is the most effective. The balance between the methods will be affected by many factors, including the age and ability of the class and their general attitude and response to their teacher. With experience the teacher learns to vary the method used according to the needs of the moment and the effectiveness or otherwise of what is being done. It must be remembered that the work is very limited if one method is used all the time. The richness and the success of the work depends upon the intelligent use of all methods.

The Direct Method

We have already explained that in Direct teaching the choice of what is to be done is made entirely by the teacher. This method has become unpopular in some circles because it is said to be non-educational. This view is based on the opinion that there are no opportunities for exploration, invention and initiative, that it is a 'pouring-in' rather than a 'bringing-out' process and that in general there is too much imposition of adult-chosen activities. Moreover it is said that there is little opportunity to cater for the needs of those children who are physically above or below the average. In other words, it is difficult to cater adequately for children of varying physical ability and, especially when using large apparatus, confidence can be seriously undermined.

31

All these points are justifiable criticism of the Direct Method, and we subscribe to them all. On the other hand there are indisputable factors in its favour and, by enlarging on these, we hope that teachers who use this method will be encouraged by the knowledge that what they are doing is not entirely wrong.

(i) In the first place the Direct Method enables some teachers to establish themselves as far as discipline is concerned, thereby giving both teachers and children a sense of security. This method is more suitable for some teachers in the early stages of their teaching career. When transferring from the Direct Method to the Indirect, it is wise to do so slowly and gradually, retaining some aspects of each during the period of transition.

(ii) Activities and movements taught by the Direct Method can often provide a starting-point from which to build and develop—thus following the sound teaching maxim of proceeding from the known to the unknown.

(iii) Some activities, especially in their early stages, can best be taught as class activities (e.g. running), and it is often more effective and easier to make a coaching point to the whole class when all are practising the same activity.

(iv) It is sometimes desirable for a particular activity to be practised because of a general lack of quality in the class (e.g. lightness in landings), or because of an undisputed desire on the part of the class to practise that activity or acquire a specific skill (e.g. hand-stand, cartwheel or leap-frog), or where skill of a particular type is fundamental to success (e.g. stretching as in jumping and control as in balance).

(v) It is sometimes valuable to challenge the whole class to perform a specific movement or activity where such movement or activity is within the capacity of the class as a whole and where there is no danger element even when the child has not been completely successful. Children should not be led to suppose that they can go through life always being completely free to choose, and, if they so wish, to take the line of least resistance. They should be faced at times with a particular and specific demand.

32

9 Maximum activity is a feature of modern work

10 Large apparatus makes the work more interesting and demanding

11 Experimentation allows for the maximum development of each child's
potential ability

12 Children learn by careful observation of each other

In all aspects of school work there are occasions when children are told specifically what to do; for equally sound reasons this discipline applies just as much to the teaching and practice of Physical Education. It is our experience that sometimes children enjoy being told what to do, just as much as on other occasions they enjoy the opportunity to choose for themselves.

(vi) Perhaps the most successful way of using the Direct Method of presentation in modern work is to apply it to an individual or group rather than to a whole class. We find this being done more and more frequently.

There are many teachers today who feel that they are out of date and wrong if they resort to direct methods of teaching, because there has been so much emphasis laid on the benefits of freedom and exploration. We are sure that teachers are wise to make use of a combination of *all* methods, as and when the circumstances appear appropriate, and the blend will be an individual matter for each teacher. The key to successful teaching is confidence and conviction—it is much better to have a teacher confident and capable in the Direct Method than an insecure teacher floundering with the Indirect Method of presentation.

The Indirect Method

In this method, the children are completely free to choose their own activity or movement, with or without the use of apparatus. The values of the Indirect Method are:

(i) In the training and education of children it is valuable on occasions to allow them freedom of choice and opportunities for exploration, experimentation, for the use of imagination and for the development of initiative, inventiveness and creative ability.

(ii) The teacher is given an opportunity to discover the likes and dislikes of (a) individual children; (b) different age groups; (c) boys and girls.

(iii) There is opportunity for each child to excel and to reach a higher standard.

(iv) Each child can work and develop fully within the scope of his physical and mental ability and his physique.

(v) There is opportunity for the teacher to assess the value of the training given, by seeing what each child can do when free to choose.

(vi) Each child becomes confident in the use of the large apparatus by being allowed freedom to get used to it. We are in no doubt that this is the correct approach when introducing children to large apparatus.

Even when the child is doing all the choosing for himself, the teacher must not retire into the background but must be continually encouraging, coaching and stimulating, to obtain quality and variety from each individual child.

Some of the disadvantages of the Indirect Method are these:

(i) It can lead to a limitation of the child's repertoire. Some teachers are satisfied when each child in the class is doing something different without appreciating or realising that each child continues to do the same thing from lesson to lesson. Although this variety is a pleasing reflection of the training, it can be misleading. The variety that is really important is not the variety of the class but the variety of which each individual child is capable.

(ii) It is possible for the child to neglect the movement, activity, part of the body or piece of apparatus at or with which he is not very able or skilful.

(iii) Class coaching is made more difficult since all the children might be doing different things.

(iv) Discipline at times can be a more difficult problem, but the method or approach itself soon solves this.

The Limitation Method

This could be called the 'Middle Line'—one which takes advantage of the best in both direct and indirect teaching. It is by far the most effective method, having the values of both the direct and indirect methods while eliminating the weaknesses of each.

While opportunities for a choice of activity are presented, the choice is limited by particular factors, the children being free to practise within the limitations set. The teacher's usual difficulty is to decide what limitations should be set. It will be remembered that the teacher nominates the type of movement or activity to be practised, e.g. stretching, rolling, jumping, etc. Great variety is possible if the teacher has readily at his command a repertoire of stimuli, ideas, themes, tasks, situations, etc., which can be used.

Some of the advantages of this Limitation Method are:

(i) It allows opportunity for exploration, experimentation and the 'bringing-out' process, and is, therefore, regarded as fundamentally educational.

(ii) It allows for individual differences of physique and physical ability, and for the maximum development of each child's potentialities.

(iii) Choice is linked with direction so that both teacher and child retain a sense of security.

(iv) If the tasks are well chosen this method ensures that all aspects of gymnastics, all types of activities and all parts of the body are used, thus eliminating the dangers of one-sidedness.

(v) Coaching the whole class is possible because of a certain amount of similarity in the type of movement being practised (e.g. different kinds of jumps may be coached for common qualities of height, resilience, etc.).

(vi) It allows for progress at the individual's own rate—the gifted are not handicapped and the less gifted are not discouraged. This surely justifies the use of the Limitation Method in the teaching of Physical Education.

Combining the methods

The three methods of presentation we have outlined indicate the variety possible in the way the teacher can plan and present his work. We have already stressed the need to vary the method used and to use a combination of all methods as often as possible. Teachers should realise that one method of presentation can follow another imperceptibly.

For example, the teacher may have asked the children to practise freely with a small ball (Indirect Method). While the children are practising, the teacher might either move from one to another, coaching, commenting, stimulating and encouraging, or watch the class as a whole, observing the variety and quality of the work being done. Following this free practice the teacher might select a child or children to demonstrate a specific activity (e.g. throwing up the ball and catching it with two hands). This activity could then be coached and the children asked to practise it with the coaching points in mind (Direct Method).

i.e. FREE ACTIVITY (Indirect)
↓
SPECIFIC ACTIVITY (Direct)

On the other hand, the children may have been asked to practise a specific activity (e.g. throwing up the ball and catching it with two hands) (Direct). This could be coached and practised, demonstrations could be used and then the children asked to practise freely with their small ball (Indirect).

i.e. SPECIFIC ACTIVITY (Direct)
↓
FREE ACTIVITY (Indirect)

It will readily be appreciated that the variety of ways in which the three basic methods of presentation may be combined is considerable and a few examples will be sufficient to illustrate this feature of teaching technique.

(i)   SPECIFIC ACTIVITY (Direct)
↓
TYPE OF ACTIVITY (Limitation)

E.g. Practice of cartwheels (coach, demonstrate, etc.), followed by free practice of any movement where the weight of the body is taken on the hands.

(ii)   TYPE OF ACTIVITY (Limitation)
↓
SPECIFIC ACTIVITY (Direct)

E.g. Free practice of any movement where the body weight is taken on the hands followed by practice by the whole class of one of these movements selected by the teacher.

(iii)   FREE ACTIVITY (Indirect)
                                    ↓
            TYPE OF ACTIVITY (Limitation)

E.g. Free practice using individual mats followed by any kind of movement 'over' the mat.

(iv)   TYPE OF ACTIVITY (Limitation)
                                    ↓
            FREE ACTIVITY (Indirect)

E.g. Practice of any kind of movement using the rope on the ground, followed by free practice with the rope.

It is useful to note that the selection of the specific movement can be made either (a) through the medium of selection and demonstration of something which is already being practised; or (b) as a result of a specific request by the teacher for some movement or activity which he has previously decided he wishes the children to practise.

It must be emphasised, however, that when the whole class is asked to practise the same thing, the movement selected should be within the capacity of the class as a whole and that there is no danger element even if the child is not completely successful.

The teacher who has been accustomed to a more formal lesson and to the use of the Direct Method of presentation is well advised to use the more specific activities as a foundation from which to develop a more indirect approach. For example, after asking the children to practise a simple pat-bouncing movement with one hand, he could invite discussion and comment on the movement being practised, leading to the suggestion that:

(a) other kinds of bouncing might be practised;

or (b) parts of the body other than the hands might be used for bouncing the ball;

or (c) other kinds of movements could be practised, still using the hands only.

From experience the teacher will find that the more he uses the Indirect or the Limitation Methods of presentation, the less he will find himself inclined to use the Direct Method. This is a development which we would encourage because the work becomes so much richer, so much more individual as a result, and because the children begin to understand so much more clearly not only what they are doing but how they are doing it.

Developing an idea

We have shown how the varying methods of presentation can be combined in many different ways to provide variety and interest and to give the work greater breadth and depth. The ideas and situations created must be used and developed to the utmost, for there is much to be gained from the development of any one of the ideas or situations so created. The following sequence of training will help teachers to accomplish this:

1 Select a type of movement and ask the children to solve the task set in any *one* way.
2 Ask the children to solve the task in *other* ways:
  e.g. (a) at varying speeds,
      (b) in different directions,
      (c) with or on other parts of the body,
      (d) with the body in different positions or shapes,
      (e) by using more than one of these factors at the same time.
3 Combine some of these variations to produce a pattern or sequence of movements.
4 Arrange and perform the sequence so that each movement flows smoothly and imperceptibly into the next.
5 Add further variations or movements to the original sequence or pattern.

As an illustration of this teaching technique, let us take a simple idea and develop it in several ways as could be done in a lesson. To develop the idea fully, several lessons will be required.

Stage 1 'Get a small ball and practise any kind of bouncing.'

Stage 2 'Now, having found one way, see if you can find other ways of bouncing the ball.'

This can result from the children's experimentation or from watching others, but they should be encouraged to find as many variations as possible.

Stage 3 'Now put some of these movements together to make a pattern or sequence of different kinds of bouncing.'

Stage 4 'See if you can join the movements together to make your sequence smooth—if necessary change the order of the movements so as to link them more smoothly.'

Stage 5 'Add other kinds of bouncing practices to your sequence to make it more interesting and varied.'

How would this work in practice? What details of teaching technique are involved? The ball-bouncing sequence could be developed in the following way:

Stage 1

The teacher asks the children to get a small ball each and to practise any kind of bouncing. He then coaches individuals—making comments, giving advice, criticising or encouraging as he moves around the class seeing what is being done.

Stage 2

There are several ways of introducing this second phase.

(*a*) The teacher stimulates the class to find other ways of solving the task. For example, after asking the children to practise any kind of bouncing with the ball (Stage 1) the teacher might then say—'Having found one way of bouncing your ball can you find other ways?' (Stage 2) or 'How many different ways can you find?'

(*b*) The teacher uses demonstration and observation by

    (i) asking the class to watch individual children,

or (ii) asking the class to watch several children at the same time,

or (iii) asking half the class to watch the other half,

and to notice the variety of bouncing activities which are being shown. He then asks the children to continue practising different ways of bouncing the ball.

39

(c) This change from Stage 1 to Stage 2 can be made in another way, where, following demonstrations by different children, the class is asked to comment on those factors which produce the different bouncing movements.

E.g. (a) One child is bouncing the ball quickly, another slowly.

   (b) One child is bouncing the ball in front, another at the side or behind, while another may be moving the ball forwards or sideways.

   (c) One child is bouncing with the right hand, another with the left hand, another with alternate hands, the back of the hand or even with the foot.

   (d) One child is bouncing the ball while standing, others are in a kneeling or sitting position.

   (e) One child is moving forwards quickly, another backwards slowly; one child is standing and bouncing the ball very high, while another is kneeling and bouncing the ball very low.

Following these observations and comments, the teacher then asks the children to practise different ways of bouncing the ball—bearing in mind the various factors involved.

The richness of the variety which will be produced by this method will be directly dependent upon the knowledge and understanding which the children have acquired during the whole of their previous training.

It is recommended that teachers should make use of the three methods which have been described, i.e. (a) stimulation by the teacher; (b) demonstration and observation; and (c) demonstration, observation and comment.

The children must be given plenty of time to develop their ideas and to explore the many opportunities afforded them in Stage 2. Teachers should repeat this phase of the training frequently in order to produce more variety and a better standard of performance. It must not be forgotten that the aim is twofold—to improve quality and to increase variety.

Stage 3

Stage 3 is reached when the teacher asks the children to combine two or more of the ways they have found into a pattern or sequence which can later be enlarged and modified. Continuing to illustrate this idea from bouncing movements with a ball, a simple sequence could be evolved:

(i) By combining different kinds of bouncing movements;
(ii) By combining bouncing movements in different *positions*, at various *speeds*, in different *directions*, etc.

By using the teaching technique already described the children will learn, by observing each other, how their own sequences are developed and improved.

Stage 4

Stage 4 is a particularly interesting phase in which an even greater demand is made upon the children's skill, their imagination and their creative ability. Now they are faced with the problem of arranging or rearranging the various individual movements in their pattern and of linking them together in order to improve the continuity of the whole sequence. The children really enjoy this stage.

We ought perhaps to add that it is not essential for every idea to be developed through every one of these stages. Teachers will find variety developing naturally as a result of previous teaching and the development on the part of the children of a greater understanding of the many factors which are involved. Thus, the teacher in the Physical Education lesson will find himself being led by one idea to the next.

Stage 5

In Stage 5 the children are given the opportunity to expand their sequence or pattern by introducing other variations of the task set. Occasionally it will be advantageous to return to Stage 2 for further exploration.

We have dealt with this teaching sequence—the developing of an idea—in some detail because it is most rewarding from both the teacher's and the children's points of view. Further reference to the application of this technique to other types of activities, with or without apparatus, are made in other chapters so that it will be sufficient here to give only a few more suggestions where the teaching sequence described can be applied:

e.g. (*a*) Rolling

Stage 1 Practise any kind of rolling movement.
Stage 2 Discover other ways of rolling.
Stage 3 Combine some of the ways you have found to make a sequence of rolling movements.
Stage 4 Arrange your movements into a smooth continuous sequence.
Stage 5 Develop and expand your sequence by the addition of other rolling movements.

(*b*) Weight on the hands

Stage 1 Practise one way of taking your weight on your hands.
Stage 2 Find any other way or ways of taking your weight on your hands.
Stage 3 Combine some of these ways to make a sequence or pattern.
Stage 4 Make your sequence into a smooth continuous one by changing the order or by adding other movements to help the flow and continuity.
Stage 5 Add still further to your sequence.

Coaching

In all aspects of physical activity, at both adult and school level, there has been, in recent years, a greater stress laid on the value of coaching. As a result, all organisations related to major recreative and sporting activities have established their own coaching schemes with well-qualified coaches available to a much greater proportion of the public. In this respect we think particularly of the coaching schemes related to the major games, football, athletics, swimming, hockey, cricket, tennis, etc., and more recently to outdoor pursuits such as camping, mountain activities, canoeing, ski-ing, rock climbing, etc.

The term 'coaching' is also being used more in relation to the technique of teaching in the Gymnastics lesson where 'coaching' as such has to a very great extent replaced 'instruction'. The word has developed a fuller meaning in that we now include in our technique of coaching the many opportunities for guidance, help, encouragement, stimulation to greater effort, improvement in performance and greater variety which occur during every lesson.

To be effective, a teacher needs the ability to see which aspect of the movement requires particular attention and, if a number of aspects need attention, the ability to decide which needs to be dealt with first. Thus the development of powers of observation and the ability to use these powers critically are vitally important, as are the ability and skill to assess the more important requirements and deal with them adequately. From experience we find that teachers, generally, tend to try to coach too many things at once, with the result that the children, asked to think of everything at once, think about nothing in particular. The advantage of concentrating on one aspect of a movement or activity only, is that the children can bring their attention and effort to bear more successfully on the particular problem set for them.

Another important quality in an effective teacher is the ability to develop the child's versatility and adaptability. In addition to the need for improving the quality of performance and developing physical ability, there is also the necessity for the teacher to have readily at his command a repertoire of the stimuli, ideas, themes, tasks and situations which he might use to set the scene in which the child can produce, in movement of all kinds, the greatest wealth of variety of which he is capable, and in which he can develop powers of control and confidence to deal successfully with any situation in which he may find himself.

COACHING METHODS

There are many ways in which coaching can be successfully accomplished and teachers should develop as great a variety as possible in the methods they use so that their teaching technique does not become stereotyped. The following methods have all been found to be successful:

1 *General class coaching during practice*

While the children are actually working, the teacher will be making comments, giving encouragement and stimulating without interrupting the practice. He might say such things as:

Can you run a little more lightly?

Can you stretch still further?

Don't forget to watch the ball all the time.

Try to jump higher.

Are you thinking about good footwork?

Can you make it a bigger movement?

What other ways can you find of moving round your apparatus?

2 *Individual coaching during practice*

While the children are working the teacher moves round and gives help to individual children, stimulating the quality of the movement or encouraging greater variety. His comments would be similar to those given above except that they would be based on observation of the individual and his particular needs.

3 *General coaching following practice*

While watching the children working, the teacher might notice a particular feature of the work which requires special attention. In this instance it will be better to stop the class to make his point more forcibly and more deliberately than he could by using Method 1. He might stop the class and briefly explain his point, suggest how improvement might be accomplished, and ask the class to continue practising with this particular point in mind.

E.g. (*a*) Stop, children; I am sure you can go much higher. Try again and show me that you can. (Quality.)

Or (*b*) Stop a minute, children. I've seen some of you skipping really slowly and some really quickly—will you try to

44

show this variation of speed much more clearly than most of you are doing at the moment? (Variety.)

4 Coaching by question and answer

The teacher stops the class to make a particular point as in Method 3 above, but in this case he asks the children questions relating to what they have been doing. Having established the importance of a certain aspect or feature of the type of movement being practised, e.g. absence of lightness in landing or lack of variety in jumping, he then asks them to continue their practice, thinking of the particular point made.

E.g. 'What is one of the most important things to remember about your landing?' (Quality.)

'In what other ways could you use your body in the air?' (Variety.)

It must be stressed that this question and answer method can sometimes tend to hold up the lesson. If satisfactory answers cannot readily be obtained, it is wise to discontinue the questioning and allow the children to resume their practice.

5 Coaching by demonstration only

While the children are working, the teacher notices that certain children are showing a standard of performance or a variety of movements which he feels the class would benefit from seeing. He stops the class, asks the child or children to demonstrate and then perhaps draws attention to the movement as a whole or to a particular feature of it. Without saying anything more he would then tell the children to carry on with their practice. This looking at each other gives the children ideas and stimulates them to greater effort.

E.g. Stop, children. See how high John jumps.

Look at Mary and see how lightly she comes down.

See how well these two children 'follow through' with their hands when they catch the ball.

Look at the different ways these three children stretch and curl their bodies.

6 *Coaching by demonstration and observation*

As in 5 above the class is given an opportunity to look at a demonstration by one or more children. The class is then asked to note and comment upon certain features of what is being shown. The questions can be asked,

(*a*) while the demonstrations are actually being given:
   e.g. 'What do you notice about this?'
   'What are the differences between these two?'
   'Which part of this movement do you like best?'
or (*b*) after the demonstration has been given:
   e.g. 'What did you notice about it?'
   'What differences did you see?'
   'What did you like most about what you saw?'

The advantages of this method result from allowing the children to concentrate on what is being shown, and then on the questions which follow.

Teachers should understand that the above methods are all valuable but that there are occasions when one is more appropriate than another. They must learn to recognise these occasions and to act accordingly. For instance, it would not be appropriate when outdoors on a cold day to stop the class frequently to ask questions, or to interrupt the practices at the beginning of the lesson. The best teachers will from time to time make use of all these methods of coaching.

Demonstration and observation

The use of demonstration and observation by the children has become such an important part of a modern teaching technique that we feel it would help to give particular attention to this aspect.

DEMONSTRATION

Demonstrations are given for a number of reasons, for example:

(*a*) to show something well done;
(*b*) to show something that has been improved;

(c) to show something new;
(d) to show varying responses to the task set;
(e) to show varying styles in performance;
(f) to show similarities;
(g) to show differences;
(h) to test the 'seeing' powers of the class;
and (i) to show particular features.

When using demonstrations the teacher should be aware of certain important technical points with regard to discipline and the arrangement of the class, etc. For example:

(a) all must be able to see—it is often an advantage for the class to sit down;
(b) all must be able to hear;
(c) all must pay attention—the good teacher will not go on with the demonstration unless he has everyone's attention;
(d) demonstrations should not be given too frequently. Sympathetic though we are to the values of demonstration, we are equally certain that there is great value in uninterrupted practice during which children have an opportunity to learn from their own mistakes and profit from demonstrations they have previously seen;
(e) demonstrations should not last too long—sometimes the continuity of a lesson can be spoilt by this;
(f) the same child or children should not be used too frequently —over a series of lessons it is hoped that all children will have been used for demonstration purposes;
(g) demonstrations should be used sparingly at the beginning of a lesson, in cold weather and when children are being introduced to new apparatus;
(h) demonstrations should be followed by practice so that the lessons learnt can be applied;
(i) coaching should sometimes be done during a demonstration and sometimes afterwards;
(j) demonstrations should sometimes be used to illustrate a movement as a whole, at other times to illustrate one aspect of it;

(k) demonstrations should sometimes be carried out with one child, sometimes with two and sometimes with more (e.g. small groups, half classes, boys or girls).

OBSERVATION

One of the aims is to develop all-round ability and one way of doing this is through intelligent observation of each other. Demonstrations help to stimulate (a) a better standard of performance (i.e. to improve quality) and (b) greater variety.

It is one thing for a child to 'look at' a demonstration but quite another for the child to 'see' and 'understand'. The teacher must from time to time test the powers of observation of the children and will often find it necessary to spend some time training them to develop this ability to observe intelligently. It is sometimes necessary to direct the attention of the children to particular aspects of a demonstration, and then to ask questions about it.

E.g. 'What did you notice about Mary's jumping?'
  'Why was she so light when landing?'

In this way the children's understanding of the technique required is increased and their attention is focused particularly on improving the quality of their own work. The other important purpose of observation is to help in developing the ability of the children to assess similarities and differences in the work being demonstrated. Thus two or more children would be asked to show what they are doing and the teacher would then ask questions relating to what has been shown.

E.g. 'What do you notice about the way these two children are working?'
  'In what way (or ways) were they alike?'
  'In what ways were they different?'

Let us suppose that the two children selected were both doing a rolling movement on their mats. The children would recognise the similarity of the movement being practised.

E.g. 'They are both rolling.'

With regard to the differences, the children might answer:

48

13 Children enjoy making identical patterns

14 'Be found working not waiting'

15 The teacher selects the type of movement—balance

16 Balance—control of the body weight on small parts

(a) One rolled forwards—the other backwards. (Direction.)
(b) One was curled up—the other stretched out. (Shape.)
(c) One was slow—the other was quick. (Speed.)
(d) One started from his feet—the other from his hands. (Body part.)

Two issues are now involved:

(i) training the children's powers of observation and their ability to assess what is going on;

and (ii) encouraging the children to make use of what has been observed and commented upon, to increase the variety of their own work.

Subsequent practice would therefore be influenced by what had been shown and discussed. After such a phase in the lesson it might be sufficient for the teacher to say, 'All right, children, carry on with your rolling practices thinking about what you have just seen.' At a later stage the teacher might remind the children of some of the particular aspects of the activity which were commented upon during the previous demonstration, and stimulate them during their practice by such comments as:

Can you find other ways of rolling?
Can you roll at different speeds?
Can you roll in different directions?
Can you make different shapes when you roll?

This principle of making use of what the children have observed in others can and should be applied in all phases of the lesson. Perhaps one further example will be sufficient to make this very important aspect of teaching technique clear.

Let us assume that the children are practising freely with a small ball. The teacher notices the many different ways in which the ball is being used and decides to make a feature of selected aspects in order to emphasise the great variety which is being, and which can be, produced. Children will be selected from time to time to demonstrate and the class will be asked to comment.

Over a series of lessons when several different demonstrations have been given, some of the comments might be:

49

John is using his feet—Mary is using her hands.
Anne is bouncing her ball—Peter is dribbling his.
James's ball is used on the ground but Janet's is in the air.
George is working in a small space but Hilary is moving
   about the hall.

Any one of these various ways of using the ball can be utilised
for developing further along a specific line:

e.g. 'Anne is throwing and catching her ball—shall we *all* throw
   and catch?'
Selection of children might now be made to develop the
throwing and catching theme and demonstrations might show
that:

Anne is throwing up her ball and catching it high in the air,
   John is catching his near the floor.
Peter is staying in one place but Christine is moving about.
James is using only one hand—Carol is using both.
Jill's ball is in front of her but Alan's is at his side.
Helen is moving forwards but Ian is moving backwards.
Cynthia is doing only one movement but William has made
   a sequence of two movements.

The variety possible is almost unlimited; and the final stage is
reached when the children have developed such an understanding
of the factors which influence what they do that they produce
this great variety of their own volition without the repeated stimulation of the teacher. The personal contribution of the child is the
all-important feature which ensures the truly educational value of
the work done.

It will be seen from this chapter that there are numerous factors
involved in the successful presentation of Primary School work.
Though each factor is important we must emphasise that teachers
will differ from each other and will give varying degrees of attention to these factors. We recognise the right of each teacher to his
or her individual approach and we encourage this. Each teacher
should develop the particular technique or method which he or
she finds most successful, bearing in mind the basic principles
involved and the standards of work which are possible.

CHAPTER 4

The Lesson

The need for a lesson plan and the selection of material

In the 1933 Syllabus, as well as in those which preceded it, the scheme of work was presented in a series of lessons and tables. Each table of exercises was designed to provide material for a period of several weeks. The only choice of exercise possible was that provided by the inclusion of two or three alternatives under each section of the table, and these sections were divided largely on anatomical grounds, e.g. head and neck, trunk—lateral, abdominal and dorsal, etc.

In the modern approach to Physical Education, the need for a lesson plan, or a framework around which to build the lesson, is still essential, but teachers are now given the opportunity to draw up their own schemes and furnish the content of each lesson for themselves. In other words, the responsibility for the selection of material for the lesson and the method of presentation of this material has moved from the syllabus to each individual teacher. This is a very good thing, provided that the teacher is willing and able to accept this responsibility and the work entailed in preparation. We find that teachers generally are very willing to undertake this additional work because, although a considerable amount of direction is withdrawn, they are now given the opportunity to choose their material according to the needs of a particular class, instead of relying upon a centrally devised and somewhat inflexible scheme.

However, teachers still require guidance and help in the selection, planning and presentation of their work and we have endeavoured to give such help and guidance in various chapters of this book. The problem of the work itself is concerned with the effective selection, from all the material available, of that which is particularly suitable for any given class. The effective selection of suitable material will be influenced by one or more of the following factors:

(a) the ability of the class (this involves not only their physical ability but their understanding of what is going on);

(b) the age of the class (this is not a true guide, but younger children should be allowed the maximum amount of freedom to explore and invent);

(c) the previous training of the class (if this has been on formal lines, the change to a less formal approach will have to be made and this should be done gradually);

(d) the facilities available, e.g. size of hall, playground, etc.;

(e) the amount and type of apparatus available;

(f) the particular needs of the class, e.g. physical (such as resilience) and others (such as initiative or independence);

(g) the length of the lesson;

(h) the training, experience and inclinations of the teacher; and (i) the lesson plan.

These points serve to remind us of the responsibilities now placed on the teacher and the need for careful planning and thorough preparation, without which all lessons become stereotyped and progress very limited.

The lesson plan itself

There is still a need for a lesson plan, not only to ensure the harmonious development of all parts of the body, but also to ensure that all aspects of the work are given adequate attention. Without a guide of some sort a lesson could easily become very one-sided, and a lesson plan has been recommended at all stages in the development of the Physical Education lesson during the last fifty or sixty years. It is interesting to compare current ideas with the plan of the earlier Drill lessons outlined in the Board of Education's 1909 Syllabus of Physical Exercises, and the later publications of 1919 and 1933.

Planning the Programme, the Ministry of Education's book on

Primary School Physical Education published in 1953, emphasises the need for a 'framework' for the lesson and describes several factors which would influence the teacher in his choice of a lesson plan. It goes on to say that teachers may wish to draw up their own lesson plan, but gives the following basic pattern to help those who need guidance:

General activity
Compensatory movements
    (a) Trunk and leg movements
    (b) Arm and shoulder girdle movements
    (c) Foot and leg movements
Agility movements

It will be seen that the suggested framework is much simpler than previous ones, but that there still remains the suggestion that the work must cater for all parts of the body.

The plan we suggest has proved to be easily understood and applied and is outlined in Fig. 9, below.

The Lesson Plan

Part I		Part II
The **Introductory** phase		The **Group Work** or **Group Activity** phase to which at least half of the lesson should be devoted. As the ability and experience of the class develop, more time can, with advantage, be allocated to this part of the lesson
The **Running** **Jumping** and **Landing** phase		
Choose **One** or **Two** of these phases	The **Body Movement** phase	
	The **Weight** on **Hands** phase	
	The **Balance** phase	
	The **Class Activity** phase	

FIG. 9

Aims of Part I and Part II

It will be seen that the lesson is divided into two main parts, Part I and Part II. In the first part the children work mainly individually but sometimes with a partner, while in the second part they work in small groups, using large apparatus as much as possible. This is a simple framework which allows a great deal of flexibility in its application and affords the teacher considerable freedom in the selection of material for the lesson.

Each section of Part I represents a phase of training, and each phase is capable of development in many different ways. Because of the limited time available and the need to allocate a good proportion of the lesson to group work, it is not advisable to deal with all the phases of Part I in every lesson. Following the Introductory Phase and the phase dealing with Running, Jumping and Landing, it is suggested that a selection is made from the remaining phases of this part of the lesson (see Fig. 9). How then does the teacher proceed?

Within each of the phases he proposes to develop, the teacher should select a suitable starting-point and then present the children with opportunities for working on these ideas over several lessons —repetition being essential for successful progress. Subsequently, new starting-points or tasks will be selected within the same or different phases and the normal progress of repetition, consolidation and further development will follow. It is not essential to select new starting-points for all phases at the same time, because some ideas take more time to develop than others and these will be retained in the lesson for a longer period. Real progress involves development and improvement in both *quality* and *variety*. Too frequent changes in the challenge set will prove unrewarding from both these points of view.

Part I of the lesson is concerned with the training and development of the body, and with the child's ability to use his body in as great a variety of ways as possible. This is an essential factor for success in Part II of the lesson, where the ability developed in Part I is applied to the varying situations created by the introduction of large apparatus and by the organisation of the children into small groups. Success achieved in the second part of the lesson will be directly related to the effectiveness of the training given in Part I.

At one time there was so much concentration of effort on Part I of the lesson (the exercises!) that little or no time was available for 'group work'. Lessons often finished hurriedly at the end of Part I with a relay race and 'group work', as we know it today, was completely neglected. Recently there has been such concentration of effort on Part II of the lesson that often little or no time has been given to Part I. As a result one sometimes sees very inferior group work, largely because the children are devoid of ideas and have little or no ability to put ideas into practice. We are sure that Part I is essential if Part II is to be successful, and we recommend that equal importance should be attached to both.

GROUP WORK

The real test of the training and of the work being done is the ability of the children in this phase. The standard of performance, the variety of which each individual is capable, and the confidence and self-control of the class as a whole, will clearly indicate not only the effectiveness of the training given, but the ability of the children to apply what they have learnt.

TIME ALLOCATION

As Parts I and II of the lesson are of equal value we recommend that approximately one half of the time available should be devoted to each part. The division of Part I into six equal sections should not be taken as indicating that an equal amount of time should be devoted to each or, as stated earlier, that all phases should be dealt with in every lesson. A teacher in the 'modern' idiom will frequently find himself developing spontaneously an idea which has emerged at some point in the lesson. The time taken to develop this idea is most valuable and, although the lesson plan will have to undergo some modification as a result, this is by no means to be deplored. The plan is flexible enough to permit this, and also to permit the teacher to rearrange phases of the work according to circumstances. For example, it is often wise to return later in the lesson to a previous practice, or to an idea, consolidating or developing what has previously been done.

Continuity in the lesson

A good lesson flows easily. The children's practice should not be interrupted too frequently; every stop should be a stop with a purpose. The demonstrations, questions and other features of coaching should be so incidental that the continuity of the lesson is not interrupted by 'dead points'. Other rules which will help to maintain continuity are the following:

(a) allow enough time for each practice to make it worth while;

(b) occasionally give the children opportunity for uninterrupted practice—allowing them to learn and profit from their own mistakes;

(c) avoid frequent changes of apparatus in the first part of the lesson (use any piece of apparatus as much as possible while it is out, so that there is less need to return to the same piece of apparatus later in the lesson);

(d) avoid too frequent changing from group to group in any one lesson; instead, as mentioned already, let the children have sufficient time at each group to make their practice really valuable.

Continuity from lesson to lesson

Successive lessons should bear a distinct similarity to each other, though they should not be identical. Just as one phase of a lesson grows from that which preceded it, so one lesson should follow the pattern and content of the previous one and develop from it. Time must be allowed at all stages for consolidation and repetition and this only becomes possible if successive lessons bear a marked resemblance to each other. This applies particularly to group work, where lack of continuity from lesson to lesson seriously impedes progress. The apparatus should not be changed too frequently and only a little should be changed at any one time.

Development of a typical lesson

The teacher must first be familiar with the wealth of material which he might use and also with the framework or lesson plan which he intends to follow. He must then face the problem of finding answers to a number of questions:

e.g. (a) How old are the children?
    (b) What kind of work have they already done?
    (c) What space is available for use?
    (d) What small equipment is available, and is there sufficient of some types of equipment for the children to have one piece each?
    (e) How much large apparatus is available?
    (f) Are the children trained to work in small groups?

Having found the answers to these and other questions, he must then decide upon a starting-point. There are of course numerous ways of dealing with each aspect, each phase and each part of every lesson. The examples we give are chosen from many, too numerous to mention here. It is unlikely that teachers will start in exactly the same way.

Let us imagine that our teacher is young and receptive to new ideas, but has been trained on somewhat formal lines. His class of junior children is a mixed age group of average ability, and with previous training which allowed for some exploration and free choice. He has adequate hall or playground space, a good supply of small apparatus and one or two items of large apparatus. What might his starting-point be? We suggest working on the following lines.

PART I

The beginning of the lesson (see Chapter 5)

While the children are changing, he tells them that as soon as they are ready, he wants them to go to the hall (or playground) and, from their own basket or container, take a small ball and practise freely with it. (The small ball is suggested first because it is a familiar piece of apparatus and easily lends itself to opportunities for free choice.) When everybody is practising, he will probably need to remind the children about the effective use of the space available and will then watch them and see what they are doing. It should not take long to assess the quality and variety of the work being done. He might then decide to leave the children practising freely in this way for a short time, encouraging them all the time to improve the quality of what they are doing. It might be wise for him to do this, and to remain at this stage for several lessons and later to begin building on what the children are doing. He could then adopt one of several methods:

(a) select one of the activities which he feels is within the ability of the whole class, and ask the class to practise it;

(b) ask each child to change to another kind of movement with the ball;

(c) let several children show what they are doing, to give all the children some idea of the ways the ball can be used and then allow further free practice in the hope that some of the ideas seen will be used;

(d) select a type of activity and ask the children to practise freely within this limitation;

(e) let two children show what they are doing and ask for similarities and differences, then develop one of the ideas expressed;

(f) ask the class to find ways of varying the activity by doing it in different ways.

To go a step further, let us suppose this teacher decides to develop suggestion (a) above, selecting a particular activity for the whole class to practise, e.g. throwing up the ball and catching it with two hands. Following some free practice of this movement, the class might be asked to watch one or more children, to discuss various points relating to what is being shown, e.g. eyes on the ball, hands shaped like a cup, body under the ball, smooth follow through of the throw and the catch, and so on. This would be followed by further practice, until the teacher decides that the children are ready to be guided further. This expansion of the original idea results from questioning the class further about the throwing and catching they have just been practising and from suggestion, stimulation and limitation.

E.g. How else can you use the ball in the air?
    What part of your body can you use besides your hands?
    Can you use the ball on the ground?
    What else can you do with the ball, using your hands?
    What other ways can you throw and catch?

Any one of these ideas can be a basis for further experimentation by the children, and just as previously the teacher built on
what was being done, so he and the children can continue to build
further on the ideas produced in this last phase through the
medium of further demonstration, discussion and observation.
The variety is unlimited, provided that the children are stimulated and encouraged to appreciate the many different ways in
which any particular problem can be solved.

This aspect of teaching technique can be repeated in successive
lessons and at different points in every lesson and the technique
described applies equally when other kinds of apparatus are being
used or even when no apparatus is being used at all.

What must be made clear is that this phase of the lesson lasts
only two or three minutes. It must be understood that the suggestions which we have just outlined will provide sufficient
material for many lessons. The teacher must ring the changes in
these introductory practices as and when appropriate, i.e. he takes
the ball practices for a few lessons, changes over to ropes or some
other small apparatus, or sometimes to practices with no apparatus
at all, and then later returns to small balls, etc.

What happens next? This young teacher might now say: 'Put
the balls away and show me how well you can run.'

Running and jumping (see Chapter 6)

This brings him to the next phase of the lesson where he begins
to coach the class in a good running style and in general all-
round running ability. Though we are here suggesting that the
next practice might be running, it could of course be one of many
other activities.

It should be mentioned in passing that his instructions to the
class should be twofold, telling them:

(*a*) to stop what they are doing

AND

(*b*) what to do next.

The operative word is 'AND', which is followed immediately by information about their next practice. This helps considerably to maintain the flow of the lesson and this technique should be followed throughout.

A short time should be spent on this phase of running training, building on what the children are doing and on what help and coaching they obviously need. Thus there may be concentration on the use of the space, on changing direction or speed, on lightness or on good use of the feet and ankles, etc. It must be emphasised, however, that the children will benefit most by concentrating on only one aspect of running training at any one time. It will be clearly seen that, just as ideas emerge from the ball practices, so the running practice could lead to:

(*a*) other kinds of running, e.g. round or between apparatus, in different directions or at various speeds;

or (*b*) other ways of moving on the feet, e.g. hopping, bounding, hurdling, jumping, etc.;

or (*c*) moving on other parts of the body, e.g. hands and feet, hands, etc.;

or (*d*) running, combined with other ways of moving.

All these ideas lend themselves to further coaching and development, including the use of demonstration and observation of each other's efforts. The running phase might also include movements and activities which encourage foot and ankle mobility and the ability to relax.

The running phase leads to the jumping phase and in the early stages we suggest that it would be wise to introduce this work with the use of small apparatus, e.g. individual rubber mats, small wooden blocks, hoops, or ropes. In this particular instance we are suggesting that small mats should be used because we plan to continue using them in the next phase of the lesson. We would recommend that our teacher should now ask the children to take a small mat from their own corner (tray or pile) and to practise freely. This gives the teacher a chance to see what the children do on their own. Following this free practice he might then ask the class to practise jumping over the mats, or alternatively he might select a few children who are already doing this type of movement to show what they are doing, and then ask the rest of the class to practise on similar lines. At this stage the type and kind of jump they do is entirely their own choice, but coaching is necessary and the coaching points made will be applicable to all the children, e.g. lightness, resilience in landing, greater height, etc. This should provide enough work for several lessons and demonstrations should be used to develop greater variety and improved quality in performance, in preparation for the further developments outlined in Chapter 6.

Body movements (see Chapter 7)

It is the intention in the specimen lesson(s) we are describing to continue using the small mats for most of Part I, so, after giving time for some consolidation of the jumping practices, the teacher now moves on to the next section, or phase, of the lesson—body movement. The variety possible is considerable, but for the purpose of this particular lesson we suggest that the teacher might now ask the children to practise any kind of rocking movement on the mats. This phase can be developed in terms of either quality or variety. We would recommend that each child should be encouraged to improve the quality of the movement he or she has chosen and the teacher might make such comments as:

'Can you make it a bigger movement?'
'What part of your body can you use to help you?'

In addition to this general stimulation he would also choose children who are being particularly successful to demonstrate what they are doing. Later he could encourage variety by such remarks as:

'How else can you rock?'
'On which other parts of your body can you rock?'
'Can you find ways of doing your rocking differently?'

Again, just as we can coach for quality by the use of demonstration, so also can we increase and develop greater variety by the observation and analysis of one another's efforts, noticing and commenting upon such details as:

(a) the parts of the body on which the rocking is being done;
or (b) the speed of the movement;
or (c) the direction of the movement;
or (d) the shape of the body while the child is rocking, etc.

If time permits the teacher could now include a body movement of another type, such as curling and stretching, rolling, or movements on the shoulders, before passing on to the next phase of the lesson.

Weight-bearing on the hands (see Chapter 7)

Here it would be sufficient for the teacher to say, 'Practise any movement where your weight is taken on your hands.'

A number of lessons can be spent in exploring the possibilities of this idea, allowing different children to show what they are doing and allowing time for children to try out different movements for themselves. This will help the children to develop confidence in their own ability to support their body weight in this way. Later there will be opportunities to develop greater variety, to link these movements with others and to improve quality and control.

Class activity (see Chapter 7)

A young teacher will probably find that there has been quite enough to do in the lesson without including a class activity, but when time allows there are many ideas which can usefully be employed here and which are closely related to some aspects of the group work which follows.

e.g. (a) rolling practices on individual mats;
(b) individual practices with various types of small apparatus, e.g. playbats and gamester balls, blocks and canes, ropes, hoops, etc.;

(c) small group practices (not more than four per group) with large balls, with playbats and gamester balls, or ropes.

Group work

We shall deal in considerable detail with the organisation and development of group work in Chapter 8, and it will be sufficient here to give a few suggestions only. The choice will be influenced by the space and apparatus available but since we decided that this teacher had reasonable facilities and a certain amount of both small and large apparatus we suggest that his group work might be organised something like this:

Group 1 *Small balls*
    Individual practice.
Group 2 *Two wooden blocks and a 4 ft cane per 2 children*
    Ways of moving over the cane.
Group 3 *Climbing frame*
    Free practice—later, ways of stretching and curling.
Group 4 *Ropes*
    Individual, partner or group skipping.
Group 5 *Large balls (1 ball between 2)*
    Partner practices—free choice.
Group 6 *Two large rubber mats*
    Rolling movements, individual or with a partner.
Group 7 *Sloping bench on a trestle, with a large mat; a second bench and several small mats*
    (a) ways of moving up the bench, to jump from the bench (free choice);
    (b) activities from or along the bench and free practice on the mats.
Group 8 *Hoops on the ground*
    Ways of moving round or over the hoop.

63

We have described a typical lesson or series of lessons and for record purposes the teacher's plan would look something like the following:

PART I

1 THE BEGINNING OF THE LESSON

(a) Free choice—with small balls (i.e. 1 ball each).
(b) Throwing and catching with both hands.
(c) Other ways of catching.

2 RUNNING AND JUMPING

(a) Free running practice (coach for style, etc.), followed by free choice of activity on individual mats.
(b) Free jumping practice over mats (coach for lightness, height, etc.).

3 BODY MOVEMENTS

(a) Free choice of any kind of rocking movement (general coaching).
(b) Other ways of rocking.
(c) Stretching and curling.

4 WEIGHT-BEARING ON THE HANDS

(a) Free choice of movements taking the weight of the body on the hands.
(b) As in (a) but moving over or round the mat.

CLASS ACTIVITY

With a cane on two blocks for every two children—jumping and landing practices.

64

17 All the children work on their shoulders

18 Free choice of activity using a mat

19. Climbing, balancing and hanging – natural activities

20. Symmetrical and asymmetrical positions

GROUP WORK

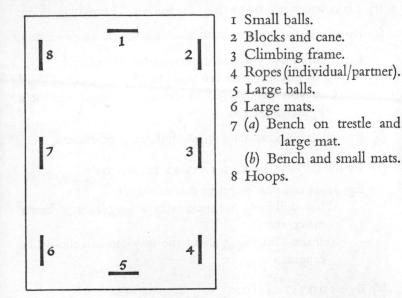

FIG. 10

1 Small balls.
2 Blocks and cane.
3 Climbing frame.
4 Ropes (individual/partner).
5 Large balls.
6 Large mats.
7 (a) Bench on trestle and
     large mat.
  (b) Bench and small mats.
8 Hoops.

Suggestions for further development

Whatever is done in the lesson, whether it be exploratory, practising a specific movement, or practising a particular type of movement, sufficient time must be allowed over a series of lessons for repetition, consolidation and improvement both in quality and in variety. Ideas alone are not enough; they must be translated into action of a worthwhile and satisfying nature. There is a tendency to think that children can go on exploring and experimenting all the time—this is neither practicable nor desirable, and the following hints should help teachers to be more demanding in their attempts to improve the standards of performance and the variety of the work.

P.E.—5

Improving the quality of performance

How can this be done?

1 By REPETITION and PRACTICE—this is a feature of every learning process.

2 By COACHING and HELP from the teacher. This may be done:

(*a*) By TEACHER STIMULATION—while the class is practising.

E.g. Think how you can improve your movement.
How much higher can you jump?
Can you make your movement a bigger one or a lighter one? etc.

(*b*) By TEACHER STIMULATION—following practice.

(*c*) By the QUESTION AND ANSWER TECHNIQUE.

E.g. How can you improve this movement?
What will help to make this a bigger or a better movement?
Tell me something about the way the ball should be caught.

(*d*) By DEMONSTRATION.

E.g. Look how beautifully Mary jumps.
Observe how well John uses his feet.
Notice how Paul follows through in his catch.
Watch how smoothly Helen moves from one movement to the next.

(*e*) By OBSERVATION, i.e. demonstration with questioning.

What helps Peter to land lightly?
What about Susan's body in the air?
Why do you like John's movement?
How did Jean improve what she was doing? etc.

The questions can be asked during or after the demonstration.

(*f*) By the use of TEACHING AIDS.

E.g. How does the rocket leave the ground?

'Squash' as you land.
Get under the 'umbrella' of the ball.
Roll like a ball.
Rock like a boat.

3 By CONCENTRATION on one aspect of the movement being practised.

Hold your *balance* a little longer.
Think about your *feet* as you move.
Concentrate on a *stretched* position of your body as it moves in the air.
Concentrate on the *lightness* of your landings.
Concentrate on the *last* part of your catching movement, etc.

4 By giving PRAISE and ENCOURAGEMENT wherever and whenever possible.

5 By DEMANDING THE BEST that each child can give.

Obtaining variety

The variety that matters is the variety of which each individual child is capable and not the variety of the class. The opportunity for each child to use all kinds of small and large apparatus, as well as the body itself without apparatus, and all these in a variety of ways, should be encouraged. In this way the child becomes versatile, adaptable, and able to deal with all kinds of physical situations confidently and efficiently.

How is variety obtained? There are six basic methods.

1 Through OPPORTUNITIES for EXPLORATION and EXPERIMENTATION.

2 By TEACHER STIMULATION.
This method off-sets the danger of children always practising the same activity or movement and is applicable to:

(*a*) The Indirect Method of presentation where the children have a *completely free choice* in what they do, and

(*b*) The Limitation Method of presentation where the children have *some choice* in what they do.

Examples of the comments the teacher might make when the Indirect Method is used are the following:

(i) Don't always choose the same piece of apparatus.
(ii) Show me how you can use your apparatus in some other way.
(iii) Try not to repeat yourself all the time.
(iv) Now practise something different.
(v) Select one movement and try to change it in some way.
(vi) How can you vary what you are doing?
(vii) Can you use your apparatus with another part of your body?
(viii) Can you use your apparatus in different ways?
(ix) Can you vary the speed of your movement?
(x) Are you able to change the direction of your movement?
(xi) Can you change from one movement to another?
(xii) What can you add to the movement you are now doing?
(xiii) How many different ways can you co-operate with a partner?
(xiv) Can you make a sequence of movements? etc.

The following are examples of comments the teacher might make when the Limitation Method is used. It should now be realised that the children's freedom is limited by the nature of the task imposed upon them. Exploration is a feature of this method, and it is important that children should be encouraged and stimulated to solve the problems set in more than one way.

E.g. Running
(i) How many different ways can you run?
(ii) How can you change your running movement?
(iii) Can you make a sequence of running movements?
(iv) Can you change the speed of your running?
(v) Can you change the direction of your running?

Jumping
  (i) Practise any kind of jumping and landing movement.
       (E.g. with a block, hoop, mat, rope, or without
       apparatus.)
  (ii) Now find another way of jumping.
  (iii) Think of ways you can vary or change your jump.
  (iv) What can you add to your jumping movement?
  (v) Can you make different shapes with your body in the
       air?
  (vi) Can you jump in different directions?
  (vii) Can you change your direction as you jump?
  (viii) Can you make a sequence of jumping movements?
  (ix) Practise a jump moving over your apparatus.
  (x) Practise jumping moving round your apparatus.

The operative words in this teacher stimulation method are:

Can you VARY your...................... movement
Can you ADD to your .... movement
Can you make a SEQUENCE of............ movements
Can you find ANOTHER WAY of doing your   movement
Think how you can CHANGE your .... movement
Now practise a DIFFERENT................ movement

3 By DEMONSTRATION.
  (a) Demonstration by one child, e.g. 'Look at the way John is
       using his apparatus.'
  (b) Demonstrations by two children, e.g. 'See how differently
       these children use their apparatus.'
  (c) Demonstrations by a group of children, i.e. observation of
       the various ideas expressed.
  (d) Demonstrations by half classes, by boys only, or by girls
       only.

4 By OBSERVATION of other children through the medium of
  DEMONSTRATION. This method is linked with the question
  and answer technique where comment is invited on the
  movement or movements demonstrated. For example:

69

(*a*) the type of movement (e.g. stretching, jumping, rolling, etc.);

(*b*) the part of the body being used (e.g. the hands, the feet, etc.);

(*c*) the part of the body taking the weight (e.g. on the hands, on the shoulders, on feet and hands, etc.);

(*d*) the speed of the movement (e.g. quick, very quick, slow, etc.);

(*e*) the direction of the movement (e.g. forwards, backwards, etc.);

(*f*) the body shape or position (wide, long, bridge-like, etc.);

(*g*) the use of space (e.g. high, low, moving about, over the apparatus, round the apparatus, etc.).

This method is most effective when the demonstrations are given by

(i) one child only;

or (ii) two children demonstrating at the same time;

or (iii) two children demonstrating—one following the other.

In (ii) and (iii) comments on the similarities and differences will be made.

5 By a REALISATION and UNDERSTANDING of the factors which, to a greater or lesser degree, influence all movements, e.g. speed, direction, shape, etc.

6 By LIMITATION—where the children are free to select, invent or explore within the limitation imposed upon them by the teacher.

It will be seen that the limitation imposed upon a class is based on seven considerations:

(*a*) Types of MOVEMENTS and ACTIVITIES, e.g. throwing, bouncing, skipping, rolling, twisting, stretching, etc.

(*b*) The PREPOSITIONAL use of apparatus, e.g. on, over, round, against, through, off, up, down, along, across, etc.

(c) The PART of the body upon which the movement is performed,

e.g. on hands, feet, shoulders, hands and feet, etc.;

and the PART of the body with which the activity is performed,

e.g. with the hands, with the feet, etc.

(d) The SHAPE of the body,

e.g. wide, bridge-like, long, etc.

(e) The relationship of the movement to the SURROUNDING SPACE,

e.g. high, low, in the air, on the ground, in a limited space, on the move.

(f) SPEED,

e.g. at different speeds, changing speed.

(g) DIRECTION,

e.g. in different directions, changing directions.

It will be seen that two or more of these can be used in combination.

E.g. 'Can you take your weight on your *hands* (body part) and make your body *stretch* and *curl* (a body movement)?'

or 'Can you *bounce* (type of movement) your ball on the *move* (use of space) and change your *shape* or *position* (body shape) as you move?'

Assessing progress

Earlier we discussed a typical lesson and we could outline many more lessons suitable for our imaginary class. We consider that this is not necessary here, because by using the methods we have described any teacher should be able to modify and adapt the lesson to suit children of different ages, of differing abilities and in different circumstances. Each teacher should build up a scheme to suit his own class, based on the work described in the various chapters of this book, and each lesson will change slightly from day to day, as he finds answers to some or all of the following questions:

1 Is the apparatus dispersed for quick distribution?

2 Are the children trained to collect apparatus from a specific basket, box or place?

3 Are the children trained in the drills necessary for the handling and care of apparatus?

4 Do the children leave the classroom knowing exactly how to start the lesson?

5 Is there sufficient continuity from lesson to lesson allowing time for repetition, consolidation and the development of new ideas? (Sometimes free—sometimes with limitation—sometimes specific—sometimes with and sometimes without apparatus.)

6 Does the class work quietly and can the children work independently?

7 Are the children using the space available to the best advantage?

8 Are the children given every opportunity in the lesson for free practice?

9 Are the children encouraged to practise something immediately they have collected their apparatus?

10 Are the children really extended and worked hard?

11 Are the children able to get to work quickly?

12 Are the children able to change from one activity to the next without fuss and noise and without unnecessary waste of time?

13 Are children used wisely for demonstration purposes?

14 From lesson to lesson, are all children used for demonstration purposes and not always the same ones?

15 Are demonstrations of the right duration?

16 Are the children getting into the habit of 'looking' and 'listening'?

17 Are the children given sufficient opportunity to comment on what they see?

18 Is sufficient time allowed for the practice of any one activity to make that practice worth while?

19 Are the children beginning to appreciate the importance of good footwork?

20 Are the children improving in their understanding of the movements and activities they are practising?

21 Is there sufficient opportunity for partner co-operation?

22 Do the children have sufficient opportunity in the lesson for free choice of activity and for exploration and experimentation?

23 Is sufficient time devoted to group work?

24 Are landing practices in the first part of the lesson applied to the activities practised in group work?

25 In group work is the space used to the best advantage?

26 In group work is the available apparatus used to the best advantage?

27 In group work are the children given sufficient to do?

28 In group work is there sufficient variety?

29 In group work is the introduction to large apparatus quite free?

30 In group work is large apparatus used near where it is normally kept?

31 In group work is there a balance between the Indirect and Limitation Methods of presentation?

32 In group work are the children trained to change from group to group with the minimum of formality?

33 In group work are the children sometimes given the opportunity of watching another group at work?

34 Is the standard of work improving and are the children becoming more interested and enthusiastic?

35 Do the children change into suitable P.E. clothing to enable them to gain maximum benefit from their work?

36 Are the children allowed to make the maximum progress of which they are capable?

Outdoor lessons

If a school does not possess indoor facilities for Physical Education, then, of necessity, lessons will be less frequent, continuity will be difficult to maintain and, unless the weather is unusually kind, standards and progress will suffer. Even in these circumstances, however, the work we have described in this book has proved to be extremely successful. We strongly recommend that even when indoor facilities exist children should be given outdoor lessons when the weather is suitable, especially in the summer months. The problems of poor playground surfaces have to some extent been overcome by the use of individual mats, and the problems of using apparatus satisfactorily outside have been solved by providing a variety of containers for small apparatus, by providing large apparatus which is portable and can easily be carried outside, and by providing fixed apparatus of various kinds in the playground.

The suggested lesson plan can be used successfully for both indoor and outdoor lessons, but the actual content of the lessons will have to be modified to suit the particular circumstances. For instance, the greater space available in a playground will enable the class to enjoy much more freedom of movement than is possible indoors, and many activities can be introduced which are not possible indoors because of limited space. A few examples are:

1 Individual ball practices which require a larger space to be really successful,

e.g. (a) throwing and catching practices on the move,
  (b) bouncing and catching practices on the move,
  (c) fielding and bowling practices;

2 Partner practices with small or large balls—aiming, shooting, dribbling, etc.;
3 Hitting practices with playbats and balls (individual, partner and group);
4 Skipping on the move;
5 Many running and jumping practices;
6 Chasing games and games practices of all kinds.

The outdoor lesson will therefore assume a more recreative and gamelike form and the activities suitable for such a lesson will replace much of the more specialised training and coaching which will have been stressed during indoor lessons. Teachers with both indoor and outdoor facilities need to prepare their lessons with both facilities and weather conditions in mind.

74

CHAPTER 5

The Beginning of the Lesson

General considerations

The lesson begins with a short period of free practice of interesting and worthwhile activities either with or without apparatus. The practice may have to be directed at first, the particular activity to be practised being named by the teacher, but later the children may be allowed to select their activity from one or two alternatives and as time goes on they can be given the opportunity of a completely free choice. Their repertoire of interesting, purposeful activities will grow rapidly and the children will very quickly learn to practise successfully on their own.

This part of the lesson must make the fullest use of the time available and will clearly reflect the discipline and previous training of the class. The teacher may be busily engaged in matters of organisation, apparatus, etc., and the children should have the ability to work effectively on their own and, in time, to exhibit a degree of initiative and independence.

The teacher must have a very clear standard in mind and must not remain in the background but should pass from child to child, giving hints, criticising, encouraging, coaching and making suggestions as and when necessary. The aim of this part of the lesson is to give the child an opportunity to increase his individual ability and to widen his experience in all types of activities and movements, both with and without apparatus, but there must be a conscious effort on the part of the teacher and the child to understand the purpose of these practices and to aim at an improved standard of performance. The chief feature is that the lesson begins with activity, which is important because it sets the tone and tempo of the whole lesson. This section should merge imperceptibly into what follows. A lesson very rarely recovers from a bad start.

Good demonstrations by the children of interesting activities are valuable, but the practice of activities in which the children should each day become more skilful is the main object of this section of the lesson, which lasts only a few minutes. Demonstrations at this stage, therefore, should be less frequent than during other parts of the lesson.

Care must be taken to guide the child who always seems to practise the same activity or who continues a particular practice too long, while the lazy or slow child must be given extra attention and should occasionally be asked to demonstrate.

As soon as the children are changed and ready they should be allowed to start work on their own. The lesson starts when the first child arrives, not the last one, for the whole purpose of this part of the lesson is lost if all the children have to wait until the last child is ready. They should leave the classroom knowing exactly how to start, otherwise much valuable practice and time can be lost.

Before the lesson starts, therefore, the teacher must decide:

(a) whether apparatus is to be used or not;
(b) whether choice of apparatus is to be free or whether the children should all use the same kind of apparatus;
(c) whether to direct the activity, or to give the children a limited or a completely free choice;
(d) whether the children are to work individually or with a partner.

Ways of beginning the lesson

The teacher will discover that the lesson can begin in one of several ways.

I THE TEACHER SELECTS THE APPARATUS AND THE ACTIVITY (Direct Method)

In this method the children are told to use the same kind of apparatus (e.g. a small ball) and to practise a specific activity nominated by the teacher. This method is only practicable with sufficient apparatus for all the children to have one piece each, or for the class to practise in pairs, or for an alternative piece of apparatus to be available for the activity selected—see Example (*b*).

Examples

    (*a*) Throwing and catching with a small ball using both hands.
    (*b*) Leap-frog jump over a wooden block (boys) or over a knotted rope (girls).

2   THE TEACHER SELECTS THE APPARATUS AND INDICATES THE TYPE OF ACTIVITY (Limitation Method)

In this method the children all use the same kind of apparatus but their freedom is limited to a type of activity determined by the teacher.

Examples

    (*a*) A skipping rope each—any kind of skipping.
    (*b*) A rubber mat each—any kind of rolling.

3   THE TEACHER SELECTS THE APPARATUS AND THE CHILDREN CHOOSE THE ACTIVITY (Indirect Method)

In this method the children use the same kind of apparatus but practise any activity of their own choice. As in Method 1, the children should have a piece of apparatus each, unless this is not possible because of the shortage of apparatus, in which case the teacher could resort to alternative pieces of apparatus for boys and girls respectively—see Example (*b*).

Examples

    (*a*) Practise any activity with a skipping rope.
    (*b*) Boys—practise any activity with a small ball.
          Girls—practise any activity with a hoop.

4   THE CHILD CHOOSES BOTH APPARATUS AND ACTIVITY (Indirect Method)

In this method all the small apparatus could be used, e.g. blocks, hoops, etc., and in addition the large portable equipment could be made available, such as benches, jumping boxes, trestles, large mats, climbing frames, etc. It will be appreciated that not only is the use of large apparatus extremely popular with the children, but the practice and experience gained will also have a valuable impact on the standards obtained and the ideas produced in group work.

Though the teacher should ensure that the children, over a period, use all the different kinds of apparatus, there are advantages to be gained from encouraging them to use the same apparatus for a number of successive lessons. It is not advisable, however, in any one lesson, to allow the children to keep on changing their apparatus, but rather to encourage them to retain it so that their practice lasts long enough to be worth while. Whenever a change of apparatus is made it should be at the teacher's discretion and not just at the whim or fancy of the child who may be changing for no good reason at all.

Teachers should avoid changing the apparatus too frequently and should be guided by the amount of real work done and not by the number of times the children have changed their apparatus.

The aim should be to familiarise the children with each type of equipment and to encourage a wide variety of activities. Over a period of time the variety produced and practised by the individual is more important than the variety shown by the class at any one time. For example, it would be possible to find each child in a class practising a different type of activity or movement, but if the same kind of activity or movement is performed by the same child in every lesson the repertoire and experience of the individual become extremely limited.

It will be observed that in the list of apparatus recommended for use in this section only portable items have been included. It has been found that the use of fixed apparatus in this part of the lesson is not always practicable, for several reasons:

(a) The children are 'warming up' at this stage and should not be encouraged to undergo very strenuous work.
(b) Congestion of a number of children at one piece of apparatus leads to inactivity and possible danger.
(c) There is not always time at this stage in the lesson to get out or put away any large apparatus, particularly of the fixed type.

5 NO APPARATUS—THE TEACHER SELECTS THE
      ACTIVITY (Direct Method)

In this method the children are told to practise a specific activity without apparatus.

E.g. The whole class practises a cartwheel.

One of the advantages of Methods 1 and 5 is that any coaching hint or demonstration is applicable and helpful to the whole class and, in addition, in the early stages of this work this way ot beginning the lesson provides a satisfactory starting-point for developing a much more individual approach.

6 NO APPARATUS—THE TEACHER INDICATES THE TYPE
      OF ACTIVITY (Limitation Method)

This method allows some choice and variation within the limits set by the teacher.

Examples

(a) Practise any kind of activity where the weight of the body is taken on the hands.

(b) Practise different ways of moving about the hall.

(c) Combine a jumping movement and a position of balance.

7 NO APPARATUS—THE CHILD CHOOSES THE ACTIVITY
      (Indirect Method)

In this method the children are allowed an entirely free choice of activity without apparatus. This method is most successful if the children have had the opportunity of practising activities as outlined in Methods 5 and 6. In this way their repertoire and skill will be developed and increased.

Although we have summarised the methods of presentation possible it should be realised that at the beginning of any lesson more than one method can successfully be used. The technique of combining the methods is dealt with in more detail in Chapter 3 (Teaching Method) and teachers will find themselves developing more and more successfully the ability to build on what is being done by varying and combining the methods of presentation.

79

For example, following free practice with a rope, the children could be asked to use the rope *on the ground*, or to place the rope on the ground and practise ways of going *across* it. Additional examples of this technique have been given in Chapter 3.

Use of apparatus

If the apparatus is ready beforehand much time will be saved during the lesson. If the apparatus is not out the first three or four children ready should put it out. In many schools the monitor system is used with considerable success in this respect. The apparatus monitors are responsible for putting out the apparatus at the beginning of the day and returning it to its storage position at the end of the morning or afternoon session as required. The teacher must make sure that the apparatus is dispersed and ready for use and that the children return the apparatus neatly to its original position when they have finished using it. Each child is equally responsible for the tidiness of the apparatus after it has been used.

When using apparatus, children should be trained:

(*a*) to collect their apparatus quickly,
(*b*) to find a good space in which to use it,
(*c*) to decide quickly what to do,
and (*d*) to practise as well as they possibly can.

Beginning a lesson with a new class

Experience has shown that perhaps the most effective way of beginning a lesson with a new class is at first to use small apparatus, and in particular those pieces of apparatus with which the children are normally already familiar, e.g. small balls, bats, ropes.

Of these the small ball is particularly suitable because even in the very early stages of developing this kind of work no child will be at a loss when asked to 'Practise quite freely, using a small ball.'

The ball will immediately be used in a variety of ways and the activities and ideas thus shown can be used by the teacher in later lessons.

21 and 22 There is a place for both individual and partner
work at the beginning of the lesson

23 Running—'Use all the space'

24 Jumping and landing—moving about the hall

When the apparatus used is not particularly familiar to the children, they must be given some guidance in the way it is to be used, so that they will have a foundation on which to build and, later, a repertoire from which to select when a free choice is allowed. For example, when using a wooden block for the first time the children might be asked to practise jumping over it. This can be developed later into other ways of moving over the block, or round it, etc., and so by careful coaching and use of demonstrations a wider repertoire will be developed.

This point applies even more particularly when no apparatus is being used. It has been found that if teachers begin the lesson by asking the children to practise freely without apparatus too early in their experience of this work, the response is often very disappointing. It is recommended that such demands should be made only after there has been some training in the other phases of the lesson, so that the children have some experience on which to draw. This again bears out the point that the beginning of the lesson will clearly reflect the work the children have been doing in previous lessons.

Points to note about the beginning of the lesson

1 In all kinds of free practice, encourage movements of an active type, since one of the aims of this practice is to ensure an inspiring and lively start to the lesson. It will be necessary on occasions to modify the activity to suit varying circumstances, e.g. indoors or outdoors, a cold day or a warm one, the age of the children, their previous training, the availability of apparatus, etc.

2 Use demonstrations sparingly at this stage, as these, although valuable, can slow down the pace of the lesson. There is great value to be obtained from uninterrupted practice where the children profit from their own experience.

3 Allocate at least two to three minutes to this part of the lesson, particularly when apparatus is used. The practice should be long enough to make it worth while.

4 Continuity from lesson to lesson is essential, so that this part of the lesson can constitute a phase of training, e.g. ball work,

skipping, development of patterns or sequences, etc. Repetition has its own virtues.

5 The teacher should spend his time coaching the children to better performance or encouraging a greater variety of activities. This can be done either on an individual or a class basis, as described in Chapters 3 and 4.

6 Encourage the children to use the space at their disposal to the best advantage. It is necessary to remind the children about this quite frequently, but guidance in the use of space is an essential part of their training.

7 It is wise to avoid having some children using apparatus while others have none. It is most disconcerting and often dangerous to have apparatus such as balls or ropes being used by some children while others are, for example, practising on their hands.

8 The teacher must vary the method of beginning the lesson in order to ensure that each individual child does, in fact, develop a wide variety. For instance, unless this is done it would be possible for a child, although given a completely free choice, to practise the same activity, or use the same type of apparatus, lesson after lesson. To avoid one-sided development the teacher must be continually demanding, stimulating and encouraging greater variety, by asking the children to practise something *different*, to *vary* what they are doing in some way, to *add* something to what they are doing, to make a sequence of several movements, to co-operate with a partner, etc.

A few ideas for the introductory phase

1 SPECIFIC APPARATUS—SPECIFIC ACTIVITY

Practise: (a) 'pat-bouncing' with a small ball.
(b) catching a small ball with both hands.
(c) 'bunny jumps' over a skipping rope stretched on the floor.
(d) throwing and hitting in pairs with a playbat and gamester ball.

2 SPECIFIC APPARATUS—A TYPE OF ACTIVITY OR TASK

Practise: (*a*) any kind of skipping with a rope.
        (*b*) any kind of jumping with a hoop.
        (*c*) any kind of bouncing with a small ball.
        (*d*) bridging and arching over a knotted rope.
        (*e*) any activity with a small ball, using your feet.
        (*f*) balancing on a wooden block.
        (*g*) any jumping activity over a partner.
        (*h*) any stretching and curling or balancing on a mat.
        (*i*) Throwing and catching in pairs, using a small ball.

3 SPECIFIC APPARATUS—FREE ACTIVITY

Practise: (*a*) With a rope (hoop, rubber mat, or wooden block).
        (*b*) With a partner using individual mats, etc.

4 FREE APPARATUS—FREE ACTIVITY

Practise: (*a*) any activity with any portable apparatus.
        (*b*) any partner activity with portable apparatus.

5 NO APPARATUS—SPECIFIC ACTIVITY

Practise: (*a*) 'squash' landings on the move.
        (*b*) 'bunny jumps'.
        (*c*) hand-standing with a partner.
        (*d*) cartwheels.
        (*e*) leap-frog with a partner.

6 NO APPARATUS—A TYPE OF ACTIVITY OR TASK

Practise: (*a*) any jumping activity on the move.
        (*b*) any activity on the move, using hands and feet.
        (*c*) any kind of movement on the hands.
        (*d*) making bridge-like shapes.
        (*e*) ways of supporting a partner's body weight.

7 NO APPARATUS—FREE ACTIVITY

(*a*) Practise any activity without apparatus.
(*b*) Practise any partner activity without apparatus.
(*c*) Devise a sequence without apparatus.

CHAPTER 6

Running—Jumping and Landing—Footwork

General comments

This type of activity is so valuable physically, and has so vital a part to play in the further development of ability in games, athletics, etc., that it is recommended that some form of running and jumping training should be given in every lesson. It is difficult to think of any aspect of Physical Education where good footwork is not essential, so this part of the lesson, which deals with practices and activities of the running, jumping and landing type, deserves special attention. Moreover, this provides an opportunity for the children to be fully extended physically, an aspect of Physical Education which is often neglected.

RUNNING

Style

It is important that training in a good running style should be given in the Primary School. In order to develop a good style, the correct use of the feet and ankles and the forward lift of the knees must be taught and regularly practised. Frequent coaching is required and children should be used to demonstrate good style. In the early stages of running training, children should be encouraged to carry their arms comfortably relaxed in order to avoid rigid and tense positions of the arms, shoulders and body. Later, when training for speed is being carried out, the children should be made conscious of the part played by the arms in helping them to run faster and to maintain balance.

Points to note in a good running style

1 Forward knee lift.
2 Good foot and ankle movement.
3 Relaxed arms.
4 Long and loose body.
5 Good pace when running on the move—not bounding or striding.
6 Overall qualities of lightness and relaxation.
7 Ease and economy of effort.

Categories

Running activities can be divided into three categories:

1 where the aim is to improve the *quality* of the movement, i.e. style;
2 where the aim is to produce *variety* in running;
3 where the aim is to introduce an element of *competition*.

1 TO IMPROVE STYLE

Style is best improved by concentrating, in the early stages of practice, on one aspect or quality of the running movement.

E.g. Concentrate on: (*a*) the quality of lightness;
(*b*) the quality of looseness or relaxation (arms and body);
(*c*) the foot and ankle movement;
(*d*) the knee action;
(*e*) the position of the body;
(*f*) the length of pace;
(*g*) the overall quality of 'style' as distinct from the speed factor or other variations.

Practices may be done:

(*a*) on the spot (including practice on individual rubber mats with bare feet) or on the move;
(*b*) around, over or between apparatus, e.g. a block, mat, hoop or rope.

As we have already indicated in Chapter 3 on Teaching Method, for many teachers, including young teachers and those who are introducing a more modern approach into their work, the Direct Method of presentation provides the starting-point from which to build. There are many running activities which are particularly suitable for class practice and which are thoroughly enjoyed by the children. With these thoughts in mind we suggest a number of specific practices which from experience we have found to be valuable during running training.

Some suitable practices

1 Free running on the spot: (*a*) with concentration on forward knee lift; (*b*) with concentration on forward knee lift and ankle stretching.
2 Slow motion running on the spot—coaching for good style.
3 Running on the spot—with variation of speed.
4 Free running for style around individual mats, hoops or wooden blocks, etc.
5 Free running for style on the move (emphasis on knee lift):
   (*a*) about the hall or playground;
   (*b*) between various pieces of apparatus, e.g. wooden blocks;
   (*c*) in different directions (no apparatus).
6 Trotting, galloping or prancing in pairs.
7 Free running for style at varying speeds.

In the early stages of training for good running style it has been found valuable to ask the children to run, first quickly and then slowly, and to appreciate the difference between the two. The children will soon discover that when running slowly they also run more quietly, and that they make much more noise when running quickly. From their own experience and from watching others they will find that the lightness and good style of slow running are dependent upon the correct use of the knee and ankle joints and a forward, but not overemphasised lift of the knee. These points should then be borne in mind, and coached regularly and systematically during practice for both style and speed; it cannot be emphasised too strongly that these practices for running training should be a feature of lessons at all ages.

2 TO PRODUCE VARIETY

This can be achieved by:

(a) observation and practice of running at different speeds either on a signal from the teacher or voluntarily;

(b) observation and practice of running in various directions;

(c) asking the children to make a pattern or sequence of different kinds of running, e.g. sideways, quickly, forwards, in one place, etc.;

(d) running round apparatus, changing direction at varying speeds;

(e) running between and over apparatus, e.g. blocks, mats, hoops, etc.

3 TO GIVE OPPORTUNITY FOR COMPETITIVE RUNNING

Activities under this heading are mainly of the running, chasing and dodging variety, including individual and small team races and relay races.

They can be included for their enjoyment and competitive value, and for practice in dodging, swerving, etc.

Recreative activities of this type are not new and still prove extremely popular with children of all ages. They can be given in both Gymnastics and Games lessons, but in order to maintain the general pace, vigour and continuity of the lesson, activities which require a lot of teaching and explanation should be avoided. This type of activity is very suitable during cold weather to give an active, energetic and stimulating start to the lesson.

Some examples

(a) Running for STYLE, SPEED and QUICK STOPPING. (Game of the 3 S's—Style, Speed and Stop.)

(b) Running interspersed with sprinting.

(c) Running and quick stopping.

(d) Running and bounding over apparatus.

(e) Running combined with jumping, landing and other activities.

(f) Changing between slow and quick running—freely or on a signal from the teacher.

(g) Free running and dodging between apparatus, e.g. mats, blocks.

(h) Line formation—first to pass a given line or object, or first to touch or pass a given line and back to place.

(i) 'Dodge and Mark'; Here! There! Where!; Couple Tag, etc.

Points to note

1 Good training should ensure that the children run well when running from one place to another even though the running is incidental; for example, when collecting apparatus or moving from group to group, etc.

2 It is advisable, especially during recreative running practices or running with the emphasis on speed, that the floor space should be cleared of apparatus and other obstructions which might hinder the movement of the children.

3 Running practices, especially those relating to speed and stamina, need not be limited to this section of the lesson but can also be included at other times, at the discretion of the teacher. This applies particularly during outdoor lessons and in cold weather.

4 If the training and coaching of running has been effectively and successfully carried out, the children will be aware of the many factors which influence their running, so that when given an opportunity for free running practice the children will automatically vary speed, make changes in direction, etc., and show an appreciation of the parts played by the body, arms, knees, feet and ankles. Moreover, an appreciation of good footwork, lightness and resilience, obtained through these practices, has a beneficial effect on all other kinds of movements, where it not only improves performance, but gives the child a sense of aesthetic satisfaction.

Teaching hints

Begin the phase of running training with free running practice either on the spot or on the move. Then ask for emphasis on some particular point or aspect. It is suggested that this be done by selecting a child or children to demonstrate, choosing those who are actually showing the particular quality to be emphasised, e.g.

lightness or variation of speed, good footwork, etc. Discuss this quality briefly with the children by means of question and answer and then let them have more practice—building all the time on what they show and what the teacher selects for special attention. In this way the free practice becomes purposeful, and the ability and understanding of the children develop rapidly. It will be found necessary, however, to remind them constantly, through comment and observation, of the many qualities and points of technique. Throughout the Primary School, frequent repetition of practices and coaching for lightness, change of speed and direction, good style, etc., will be necessary, and this should have a beneficial effect upon all aspects of the work.

Summary of running practices

The purpose of this summary is to remind teachers of the variety which is possible in this phase of the lesson.

RUNNING
- Practices 'on the spot' emphasising one or more aspects of technique.
- Practices 'on the move' emphasising one or more aspects of technique.
- Practice round apparatus.
- Practices between and over apparatus.
- Practices showing variation in speed (acceleration and deceleration of pace).
- Practices showing variation in direction on the move or round apparatus.
- Practices making 'patterns' on the move or round apparatus.
- Activities of a recreative nature.
- Dodging, etc., between, round and over apparatus.
- Activities combined with other movements.
- Activities of the team and relay type.

JUMPING AND LANDING

General comments

Jumping and landing movements are concerned with the development of the child's ability to propel himself into the air, to control his body in flight and to absorb his body weight when it comes down again. It is possible to begin these practices by using small apparatus such as hoops, ropes, wooden blocks or individual mats, thus making the practices more interesting and objective. It should be realised that the use of small apparatus, even in the later stages of the work, does not prevent advanced interpretations of this type of movement. A safety factor is also involved in the jumping and landing phase in Part I of the lesson, for confidence can be established and ability improved when opportunities are provided for coaching and practice at floor level before large apparatus is introduced in group work.

Within the limitations of the age and ability of the class, the correct technique of jumping and landing cannot be given attention too soon, and careful teaching and coaching must be followed by plenty of individual practice. The aim should be to develop spring, lightness, resilience, strength and control, as well as the ability to jump in a variety of ways. All lessons should include activities of this type because:

(a) mentally they are exhilarating—'We jump for joy!';
(b) physically they are stimulating and beneficial;
(c) they are of primary importance in learning to control the body in flight, and are basic to the development of most gymnastic movements;
(d) of their application to the many skills associated with games, athletics, diving and other physical activities.

Methods of presenting jumping

Jumping and landing practices can be presented:

1 With *small apparatus*;
2 With *no apparatus*;

3 With *human apparatus* (i.e. OVER a partner);
4 With *large apparatus*.

From time to time all these different ways should be used, the various jumping 'situations' presented often prompting new and different ideas. Initially, the children should be allowed to practise freely, for this freedom, appropriate in all aspects of the work, is not only educationally sound, but is also valuable in establishing confidence. Later the teacher should stimulate the children towards better *quality* and greater *variety*. No matter which way it is presented (1–4 above) the jumping movement will be influenced by other factors, e.g. *take-off*, *direction*, *body shape*, etc.

Technique

Good jumping demands:
1 Lightness and resilience or 'give' (this demands efficient use of the joints of the knee, ankle and foot).
2 Extension or stretch of the body, the legs (with obvious exceptions) and the feet.
3 Height, where a high arc of effort should be encouraged.

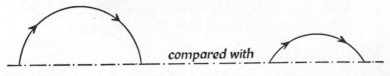

FIG. 11

It is important to realise that height in jumping cannot be obtained without a preliminary bending of the knees and ankles just prior to take-off, and that to obtain height the take-off must be quick and explosive.

4 Relaxed arms except in those jumping movements where the arms constitute part of the jump.
5 A smooth take-off when jumping on the move or over apparatus. This is made easier when the preliminary run is neither too long nor too fast.

91

Continuous jumping practices

The following practices, with no particular emphasis on the landing, are more appropriate for young children or as incidental practices for coaching special features, e.g. resilience, foot-work, etc.

WITHOUT APPARATUS

1 Free practice of any kind of jump with special emphasis on a specific quality, e.g. height, stretch, lightness.
2 The 'Bouncing Ball' type of preliminary jumping is helpful, later accompanied by a request for patterns or sequences:

e.g. (*a*) vertical (up and down);
    (*b*) horizontal (along the ground),
       e.g. shapes on the floor, letters of the alphabet, etc.;
    (*c*) a combination of (*a*) and (*b*);
    (*d*) jumping in different directions, e.g. forwards, sideways, backwards;
    (*e*) showing a change of direction, i.e. jumping with a turn of the body in the air;
    (*f*) a combination of some or all of the above.

3 Jumping with leg movements in flight.
4 Jumping with arm and leg movements in flight.
5 Jumping—making different body shapes in the air.

WITH APPARATUS

As above, using various kinds of apparatus to jump over or around, such as blocks, balls, ropes, canes, hoops, or mats.

NOTE. Variety in jumping activities can come through observation of each other's movements, from an idea expressed or limitation imposed by the teacher, or by using different kinds of apparatus; for example:

1 Practise jumping with a rope, a ball, or a hoop, etc.
2 Practise jumping around a block, or over your apparatus, etc.
3 Practise any kind of jumping with a rope on the ground.
4 Practise any kind of jumping along a rope, in and out of a hoop, showing change of body shape, etc.

Landing

It is essential that children should learn an efficient way of landing as soon as possible so that when they jump from a height they can land safely, with control, and without fear of hurting themselves. To master an effective landing much practice is required, together with careful teaching and coaching. We appreciate that there are many successful ways of landing, but the type of landing recommended has been evolved in the first instance after careful observation of children at play. When playing quite freely and jumping from a height they bend their knees fully, and if this is not sufficient to absorb the shock of impact with the ground, they roll or fall over. In addition it will be noticed that, on landing, they will invariably have their knees fairly close together. As they get older and their legs become stronger, it will be seen that the bending of the knees is followed by a quick extension or rebound and it is on these observations that the techniques of a 'squash' landing are based.

It is interesting to note that this type of landing was also used with considerable effect during the war in parachute training, and medical opinion has confirmed that it is much sounder from an anatomical point of view than the type of landing previously taught, i.e. in crouch position with knees open and with hands between the knees. The term 'squash landing' was given to this type of landing by the children themselves, being descriptive of the feeling experienced in performing this kind of movement.

This method of landing or 'squashing' must be coached. Practice will develop the necessary muscular strength and co-ordination, and good coaching, with ample opportunity for observation, will ensure the required standard of performance. Details of the position are as follows:

1 A deep bending of the knees—the body weight being taken on the ball of the foot;
2 The 'tail' sitting on the heels;
3 Knees forward;
4 The body and head held erect;
5 The arms loosely relaxed at the sides;

93

6 The 'squash', followed immediately by a quick rebound and a little jump to a standing position ('Jack in a Box').

Jumping and landing practices

WITHOUT APPARATUS

Emphasising an aspect of technique, e.g. stretch, height, 'give':
1 Off one or both feet;
2 On the move, with leg, arm, or leg and arm movements;
3 In different directions, e.g. forwards, sideways, backwards;
4 With a change of direction (i.e. a turn in the air);
5 With a partner, e.g. one child makes his body into an obstacle for his partner to jump over. This has special appeal for the older children;
6 On the move, showing a particular body shape, e.g. wide.

WITH APPARATUS

Most kinds of small apparatus already mentioned may be used here. Initially the children should be allowed to choose their own kind of jump and later to make their choice according to the stimulus or task set by the teacher.

E.g. Practise:

1 Any kind of jumping and landing over a block, a mat, a rope, etc.;
2 Jumping and landing off one foot or off both feet (later, children should be encouraged to develop the ability to jump successfully in both ways);
3 Jumping and landing, (a) showing a change of direction, or (b) in different directions;
4 Jumping and landing over apparatus showing different shapes using legs, arms, etc.;
5 Jumping and landing followed by another kind of activity, e.g. balance or by an activity taking the weight on another part of the body, e.g. the hands, shoulders, etc.

Jumping from heights (with the obvious need for greater efficiency in landing) is one of the most popular activities and is often included in group work (see Chapter 8).

This is possible from:

(*a*) benches, horizontal or inclined;
(*b*) tables, wooden boxes, or desks (if safe);
(*c*) chairs, if firmly held by a partner;
(*d*) vaulting boxes, stools, trestles, etc.

All types of jumps from a height should be encouraged, e.g.:

1 Jumps off one foot or both feet following a running movement up a sloping bench;
2 Jumps from a stationary position, e.g. standing on apparatus of various kinds;
3 Jumps with leg, arm, or body movements, in the air;
4 Jumps in different directions, or with a change of direction;
5 Jumps showing various shapes in the air, e.g. long, curled, wide, etc.;
6 Jumps, adding other activities to follow the landing, e.g. balancing, bridging, rolling—movements on hands, shoulders, hands and feet, etc.

Teaching method

Especially with young children, this phase of the work lends itself particularly to an Indirect approach and in the earlier stages free practice of any kind of jump, preferably using small apparatus, is recommended. Thus the children would be asked to practise any kind of jumping over or round a wooden block, or an individual mat, etc. All kinds of small apparatus suitable for these practices should be used from time to time, and it should be remembered that a different kind of apparatus can demand and will produce different kinds of jumps. For example, with a wooden block there will be many kinds of jumps over and around the block, but a hoop on the floor will produce 'in and out' types of jumps, as well as 'over' and 'across' and 'around'. A skipping rope used either in one or both hands, or placed on the ground to make different shapes or designs, will produce a very wide variety of jumps, all of which will evolve during free practice and free choice.

Variety will not only come from the use of different pieces of apparatus, but also from the many ideas or suggestions made by the teacher, e.g.,

'Show me different kinds of jumping around your mat; in and out of your hoop; using your skipping rope in both hands, etc.'

Children should be selected to show their jumps with a view to increasing the repertoire of each individual child, but in observing these jumps they should be encouraged to see and to discover for themselves the differences between the various jumps, so that they are able to develop their own repertoire, rather than to accept one ready made for them by the teacher.

It is necessary to develop in each child (*a*) the ability to jump in as great a variety of ways as possible, and (*b*) improved quality by an improved standard of performance.

This should be done by careful coaching, e.g.:

For variety (i) When you are jumping, what can you do with your legs in the air?

or (ii) Practise jumping in different directions.

For quality (i) How *high* can you make your jump?

or (ii) How *light* can you make your landing?

The effectiveness of the coaching depends upon the ability of the teacher to select suitable demonstrations and to use the children's powers of observation to the best advantage.

Let us suppose that the teacher has asked the class to practise jumping for height over a block. Following free practice the teacher selects two or three children to show their jumps, drawing the attention of the other children to the take-off. By questions and discussion it is established that the take-off, with its explosive character, demands the greatest effort and can be compared to a rocket shooting from the ground. The children then practise again freely, concentrating their efforts on this explosive type of take-off. By further suitable demonstrations (in this and subsequent lessons), the increased height attained will be observed; the teacher can then proceed to coach some other aspect of the jump, e.g. the stretch of the body in the air, or the lightness or 'give' of the landing. Later he might suggest that some addition might be made to the jump, e.g. leg movements in the air or a turn of the

25 'Make different shapes in the air'

26 'Use all parts of your apparatus'

27 'Show me the inverted balance you include in your sequence'

28 Ideas emerge from the 'situations' created

body before landing. A further progression is obtained by inviting
the children to add other kinds of movements or activities to their
jumps, so making a series or sequence of movements, e.g. 'After
your jump add any kind of movement where your weight is taken
on your hands.' 'Follow your jump with some kind of rolling
movement.' Great variety is possible here, and this variety should
be drawn from the children in exactly the same way as in the
previous stages, i.e. by free practice, exploration, demonstration,
observation, and further building on what has been demonstrated
and observed.

Summary of jumping practices

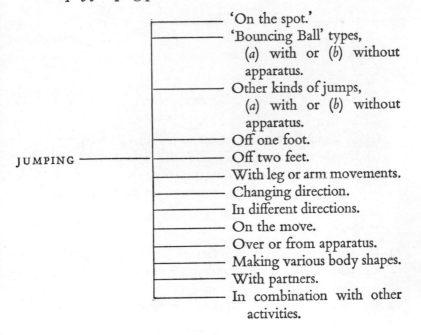

JUMPING
- 'On the spot.'
- 'Bouncing Ball' types, (a) with or (b) without apparatus.
- Other kinds of jumps, (a) with or (b) without apparatus.
- Off one foot.
- Off two feet.
- With leg or arm movements.
- Changing direction.
- In different directions.
- On the move.
- Over or from apparatus.
- Making various body shapes.
- With partners.
- In combination with other activities.

Summary of the technique of jumping

A running jump, with or without the use of apparatus, has four
parts, as illustrated in Fig. 12 on the next page.

1 The *approach*, which should be neither too far nor too fast.

2 The *take-off*, which is the low preparatory jump just prior to the jump itself. This, off one or both feet, should be 'explosive' in character. It will be seen that the knees and ankles are slightly bent to assist the 'spring' into the air. The greatest effort in the jump comes here.
3 The *flight*, which should be high.
4 The *landing*, which should be light, resilient and controlled, with an effortless rebound.

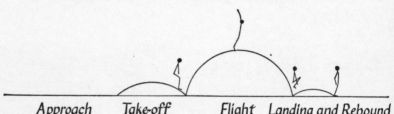

Approach   Take-off   Flight Landing and Rebound

FIG. 12

The quality of the jumping can be improved:

(*a*) by frequent practice;
(*b*) by an understanding of the technique involved;
(*c*) by observation of well-performed demonstrations;
(*d*) by concentration, during practice, on one aspect of the jump—for example, lightness, height or stretch.

Variety is obtained:

1 By an appreciation of the factors which influence the jump:
e.g. take-off, direction, standing or running, body action, leg action, arm action, body shape.
2 By the use of different types of apparatus: ropes, blocks, mats, canes, hoops, etc.
3 By observation of other children:
e.g. How is Mary's jump different from John's?
4 By increasing the limitation:
e.g. Practise jumping *off one foot.*
Practise jumping *in different directions.*
Practise jumps where you *move your legs* in the air.

5 By teacher stimulation:
  e.g. How many *different* ways can you jump?
     Now jump *another way*.

FOOTWORK

Activities for the feet and ankles

One of the fundamental features of progress towards good movement is the correct use of the feet and ankles. The aim should be to develop and maintain a full range of movement in the joints of the foot and ankle, to strengthen the muscles of the foot, to maintain the normal arch of the foot and to develop foot consciousness. Recreative foot exercises are both interesting and beneficial. In the early stages of the work, foot practices are particularly valuable, but their place in the lesson should be left to the discretion of the teacher. Although footwork practices are valuable in themselves, they will generally be included as incidental aids to the coaching of other movements. Feet should be 'light and long, loose and strong'.

Some suggestions when using footwork practices are as follows:

(*a*) Wherever possible, work in bare feet (on mats or on a suitable floor).

(*b*) Apply the practices to the coaching of running, or jumping and landing, rather than regarding them as isolated movements. The term 'long foot' rather than 'pointed toes' is helpful in making children appreciate extension of the ankle.

(*c*) Practise foot exercises for short periods only and preferably after a vigorous activity.

(*d*) Unless the weather is exceptionally good, it is advisable to restrict these practices to the indoor lessons.

(*e*) Look for children with weak or flat feet, and arrange for special attention to be given to these, either in remedial classes or by reference to the school clinic.

Teaching method

At first it is enough to ask the children to make 'long' and 'short' feet, i.e. with ankles extended and flexed, and to let them practise these movements freely and in a variety of ways, e.g. sitting, lying, on the shoulders, etc., first with one foot and then with the other.

These are best introduced as part of the coaching of the 'running and jumping' phase of the lesson by following the running or jumping with practice in making long and short feet. The running or jumping is then resumed, concentrating on good footwork, i.e. on using the ankles well.

Other valuable practices can be invented by asking the children to make big circles with their feet or to find other movements which help to make the feet feel stronger or more flexible. Younger children can be asked to tighten the feet, or curl them up and then to open them and spread out the toes; they will play at 'Fists and Fans' with tremendous concentration.

The teacher should give a suggestion concerning the type of activity required and let the children work out their own development of the ideas given. By observation of suitable demonstrations they will quickly understand what is wanted and will enjoy practising old exercises or inventing new ones.

Recreative foot activities

These are included to help those schools and teachers who are responsible for organising and conducting 'remedial' classes.

Apparatus: stocking balls, small rubber balls, marbles, beanbags, chalk, crumpled pieces of paper, skipping ropes, etc.

Teaching method

The children should first be given a chance to play at picking up suitable objects with the feet.

> E.g. 'Let me see you trying to pick up a beanbag with your foot.'

It will be necessary to point out that the objects must be grasped by the foot in a claw-like movement and not slipped between the toes and wedged there. Children should be asked to demonstrate this grasping movement and by observation and discussion they will quickly appreciate the need to 'grasp' the object in order to strengthen the foot.

A simple suggestion or stimulus will then lead the children to experiment on these lines, and to invent activities for themselves. Suitable examples should be selected to show what is being done and the children should then be given further practice during which they will attempt to apply, within their own capacity, some of the points demonstrated and suggested.

The practices should always be free and of a game-like character, but should also be purposeful. The children must learn to practise without interfering with the work being done by those around them; consideration for the others in the class is necessary and must be developed. There are many suitable activities, and the children will take pleasure in finding new ones for themselves.

In conjunction with foot exercises, teach foot cleanliness—the necessity for washing the feet daily and wearing clean socks, or stockings. Encourage the children to realise that healthy, strong and clean feet are of the utmost importance.

CHAPTER 7

Body Movements—Weight-Bearing on the Hands—Balance—Class Activities

BODY MOVEMENTS

This part of the lesson is concerned with those movements and activities which deal more specifically with the body, rather than the arms or legs.

Basically, three factors are involved:

(a) the development of the child's appreciation of the many types of movements and activities which are possible;

(b) the development of the child's ability to perform these movements as effectively as he can;

(c) the opportunities to experience as wide a variety of movements as possible.

During the practice of these activities the teacher, at least, will be aware of their anatomical and physiological values. The development of strength and mobility in all the body parts is automatically involved and the all-round beneficial effects on posture and general muscle tone, though incidental, are very valuable.

In the past, movements of the body, trunk or spine have not received the attention required. Generally speaking, children of Primary School age possess a supple spine as well as being supple at the joints of the hips and it is important that this mobility should be maintained. The tendency to 'stiffen up' can be avoided by developing and maintaining a full range of movement in all directions.

As in the case of the movements and activities included in other parts of the lesson, the necessity for repetition of activities in this group throughout the Primary School stage is important. Children enjoy repetition and the feeling that they are progressing to a better standard of performance. It should be remembered that the maximum physical benefit is derived from performing the activity really well.

If the floor surface is not suitable for some of these activities, individual mats are a great help in increasing variety and in evolving 'foolproof' activities where effort and a full range of movement are necessary.

All-round development must be ensured by using the back, front and both sides of the body, and children should be trained to apply this principle in their free practice.

Teachers should aim at a full range of smooth controlled movement; lack of control often indicates the need for more practice in relaxation. Observation of each other's movements by the children is valuable and the need for changing into appropriate clothing is obvious.

Categories

The movements included in this phase of the lesson can be selected from the following categories:

1 Movements on a particular *part of the body*, e.g. shoulders, front, back, hands and feet, etc.
2 Movements of a particular *type*, e.g. rolling, rocking, arching, stretching, curling, twisting, etc., or a combination of some of these, such as, stretching and curling, arching and twisting, etc.
3 Movements based on the *shape* factor, e.g. wide, long, curled, bridge-like, asymmetrical, etc., or a combination of some of these, such as, wide, bridge-like shapes, asymmetrically long, etc.
4 Movements based on a *combination of factors*, e.g. making wide shapes on the shoulders, twisting movements on hands and feet, rolling symmetrically, etc.

Whatever task is selected it is essential that it should be developed over several lessons and in this respect the teaching sequence, already discussed and described in Chapter 3, is recommended (see pp. 38–42). Let us, for example, consider how the task of *wide shapes* could be developed:

Stage 1 Make *one* wide body shape.
Stage 2 Find *other* ways of making wide body shapes.
Stage 3 *Combine* some of the ways you have practised.
Stage 4 Now arrange these variations into a *sequence*.
Stage 5 Can you *add* a new wide shape to your sequence?
Stage 6 Can you *rearrange* the different parts of your sequence to *improve* it?

In the later stages the teacher will concentrate on improving the quality of particular movements and on other occasions will ask the children to concentrate on improving the ways in which the various movements are linked together. It will be found advantageous to return occasionally to Stage 2 to allow opportunities for further experimentation, and so modify or enrich the sequences previously practised.

Suggestions for class experimentation and practice

1 Practise any kind of movement   (*a*) on your back;
     (*b*) on your front;
     (*c*) on your side;
     (*d*) on your shoulders.

2 Practise any kind of (*a*) rocking movement;
     (*b*) rocking movement on your front;
     (*c*) rocking movement on your back.

3 Make a sequence of rocking movements on different parts of your body.

4 Practise any kind of (*a*) rolling movement;
     (*b*) rolling movement in a curled position;
     (*c*) rolling movement in a stretched position.

5 Practise any kind of stretching and curling movement.

6 Practise any kind of twisting or turning movement.

7 Practise any kind of movement on your shoulders.

8 Practise long shapes—combine these variations.

9 Practise making bridge-like shapes and arrange into a sequence.

10 Make a sequence based on different shapes.

These are only ideas or suggestions, each of which is capable of development along lines similar to those in the example above, i.e. WIDE SHAPES. Teachers are recommended to make the fullest use of this technique, not only to enlarge the repertoire of each child but also to increase his appreciation of the many varied movements which are possible and his ability to perform them. It will perhaps be helpful to consider a few of these ideas in some detail.

Rocking

Development might be as follows:

1 Practise any kind of rocking on your back.

2 (a) Find ways of varying the type of rocking you are doing (e.g. by rocking in different directions, at varying speeds, stretched, curled, etc.).

(b) Find other ways of rocking (e.g. on different parts of the body).

3 Make a sequence of several kinds of rocking movements.

4 Join your rocking movements together smoothly.

Experimentation and coaching over several lessons will produce the following variations of rocking movements:

(a) on the back;

(b) on the front;

(c) forwards and backwards (hands near the chest);

(d) forwards and backwards (arms at the side);

(e) forwards and backwards (hands behind the back);

(f) forwards and backwards (holding ankles);

(g) forwards and backwards (arms upward);

(h) from side to side (holding ankles);

(i) from side to side (in a stretched position);

(j) changing from one part of the body to another;

(k) in various directions;

(*l*) at various speeds;

(*m*) stretched, curled, wide, etc.

Points to note

1 It is important that the children should evolve these variations by free practice, experimentation and observation.

2 A wide range of movement should be encouraged.

3 The use of the arms or other parts of the body to improve the movement should sometimes be suggested.

4 Occasionally the children's attention should be drawn (following or during demonstration) to an aspect or part of the movement, e.g. a high chest or a smooth controlled motion.

5 Rocking in various directions and on various parts of the body and at varying speeds should be encouraged.

Rolling

Children enjoy rolling movements from the earliest age and there is much value to be obtained from this type of activity. There is also great carry-over value to agility work and the practices with large apparatus in the Group Activity phase of the lesson.

Some examples of the rolling movements which will emerge

(*a*) rolling with the body stretched;

(*b*) rolling with the body curled;

(*c*) rolling from the 'bridge' (or astride) position;

(*d*) rolling in different directions (forwards, backwards and sideways);

(*e*) rolling at different speeds;

(*f*) rolling over one shoulder;

(*g*) rolling with a twist (changing direction);

(*h*) rolling from different positions and different parts of the body (e.g. from the hands, from the knees, etc.);

(*i*) rolling preceded by another activity;

(*j*) rolling followed by another activity;

(*k*) rolling preceded or followed by a position of balance.

These examples illustrate the variations of rolling movements which will emerge, but they must be allowed to emerge from the children's free practice and experimentation, assisted by teacher stimulation. In all phases of the work it is important to challenge the child's imagination as well as his physical ability.

Stretching and curling

In addition to its physical value, the ability to extend or stretch all the body or particular parts of it is fundamental to many gymnastic movements. Different kinds of stretching and curling movements can be obtained by stimulating the children to perform them from different positions or on different parts of the body.

Some suitable examples for developing these movements

1 Make yourself as small as you can—from that position make yourself as long or as tall as you can. Now practise this stretching and curling movement freely.
2 Make yourself as long as you can; from that position make yourself as small as you can. Now practise both these movements.
3 Stretch your body in as many different ways as you can. (At a later stage, encourage the children to make a sequence or pattern by combining the stretching movements they have discovered.)
4 Find different ways of making yourself as small as you can, and then find different ways of making yourself as long as possible from these positions.
5 On different parts of your body, make a sequence of stretching and curling movements.
6 Practise any activity on the move, making your body stretch and curl.

From these practices it will be seen that the children will find many ways of stretching and curling while the weight of the body is supported on their feet, back, front, shoulders, etc.

It is important to encourage the children to make their stretching movements as big as possible and in this connection the teacher should encourage the use of all parts of the body to assist the movement. The same applies to curling movements. Opportunities should also be given for practising these movements at different speeds, as well as in different directions.

Twisting and turning

It is an advantage, particularly in the early stages, to carry out twisting and turning movements from specific starting positions, e.g. kneeling, lying, on the shoulders, etc. Practice of these movements in different directions and at varying speeds is valuable in developing variety and control.

Some examples

1 On hands and knees (a) practise taking your hands for a walk round your body;
    (b) practise any twisting movement.
2 On hands and feet (a) take your hands for a walk round your body;
    (b) take your feet for a walk round your body;
    (c) practise any twisting movement;
    (d) practise any twisting movement on the move.
3 Practise any kind of turning or twisting movement:
    (a) on the shoulders;
    (b) sitting;
    (c) lying on the back;
    (d) with one hand on the floor;
    (e) in a bridge-like position;
    (f) with two hands on the floor.

During their practice the children will invent many activities, to some of which they will enjoy giving special names, for example, 'Ticking Clocks' (lying on the back, circling the legs round the body with feet on the floor); 'Windscreen Wipers' (lying on the back, swinging the legs from side to side); or 'Corkscrews' (on the shoulders, twisting and turning, while bending and stretching the legs).

In addition to the suggestions and examples already given, stimulating work is possible in this section of the lesson by asking the children to find ways of twisting their bodies round or over various items of small apparatus placed on the ground, e.g. a wooden block, a skipping rope, individual mats.

Body shape

Tasks based on BODY SHAPE are very productive of ideas, primarily because SHAPE is a common factor in all types of gymnastic movements.

Some examples of tasks based on the shape of the body

1 On different parts of your body, make a shape like a bridge.
2 Make a bridge-like shape from your (a) front;
                                (b) back;
                                (c) shoulders;
                                (d) hands and feet (etc.).
3 Make bridge-like shapes on or over your apparatus.
4 Practise making inverted bridge-like shapes.
5 Move round your apparatus making different bridge-like shapes.
6 Combine different bridge-like shapes and repeat to make a sequence.
7 Combine different bridge-like shapes on the move.
8 Find different ways of making your body shape long.
9 Make a sequence of movements based on a long shape of the body.
10 Make a sequence of different body shapes.

Movements on the shoulders

Children particularly enjoy working on their shoulders because it provides a simple but effective interpretation of body inversion.

Most of these activities are also particularly valuable for developing mobility of the hip joints.

Some examples of suitable tasks

1 Practise any kind of movement with your legs.
2 Practise any kind of cycling movement, e.g. quick, slow, with a change of speed or direction.
3 Combine different kinds of cycling movements.
4 Practise any kind of quick movement.
5 Practise any kind of slow movement.
6 Practise any kind of movement showing a change of speed.
7 Practise any kind of stretching and curling movement.
8 Practise any kind of swimming movement with your legs.
9 Practise making wide shapes with the legs.
10 Practise movements with straight legs.

11 Practise any kind of turning and twisting movement.
12 Combine different types of movements and repeat to make a sequence.

WEIGHT-BEARING ON THE HANDS

Of all phases of the lesson this is perhaps the most popular with the children, who gain quickly in confidence and strength by having opportunities to practise freely any activity of this kind. The fundamental feature of teaching these activities is to allow the children to explore, invent and make progress at their own rate and in accordance with their own ability. The activities which the children will invent are often of a recreative type, easily recognisable as the beginning of hand-standing, etc., for example 'Kicking Horses', 'Bunny Jumps'. These are then coached to produce a higher standard of performance and developed to produce a much wider variety of activities of this kind. There will also be considerable use and application of this type of movement to the large apparatus situations created in the group work phase.

Some suggested practices

1 Find ways of moving on your hands and feet.
  Variety may be obtained not only in the different activities the children will produce, but by doing these activities in different ways:
  e.g. quickly, slowly, with short steps, long steps, showing a change of speed, direction, position, etc.
2 Find ways of moving round your apparatus on your hands and feet:
  e.g. round your mat, or block, or rope.
3 Find ways of moving over your apparatus using hands and feet.
4 Practise any kind of activity taking your body weight on both hands.
5 Practise any activity where you balance on your hands.
6 Practise any activity with your hands on the mat (or floor) and your feet in the air.
7 With hands on the mat practise any·kind of running movement with your legs.

8 Practise 'Kicking Horses'. (For this activity the hands are placed on the mat and the legs are kicked high in the air.)

9 With hands on the mat practise any kind of jumping activity.

10 Practise 'Bunny Jumps', e.g. (*a*) on the mat, (*b*) over the mat, (*c*) round the mat, (*d*) with turns, (*e*) on the move.

11 How many different shapes can you make on your hands?

12 Practise any kind of hand-standing.

13 How many different ways can you come down from your hands?

14 Practise cartwheels. (All kinds of variations are possible here, e.g. quickly, slowly, with or without twist, etc.)

15 Practise 'Crab' or any similar arch-like movement.

16 'Climbing the Ladder.' (In this activity the mat or floor represents imaginary rungs of a ladder which are climbed with the hands in various ways—quickly, slowly, one hand at a time, sideways, etc.)

17 With feet and hands on the floor, take the hands for a walk in any direction.

18 Curled or stretched balance positions on the hands.

19 'Caterpillar Walk', 'Bear Walk', 'Crab Walk', 'Cat Spring'.

20 Find ways of moving about, taking your weight on your hands.

Most of these practices can be done on an individual rubber mat if the floor surface is not a suitable one.

Development in this phase of the lesson could follow the normal pattern.

For example:

1 Find *one* way of taking your weight on your hands.

2 Find *other* ways. (Variety.)

3 *Improve* what you are doing. (Quality.)

4 *Include* an activity on your hands *in your sequence.*

5 *Begin* or *end your sequence* with a movement on your hands.

6 *Combine* different ways of taking your weight on your hands.

7 Devise a *sequence* based on this idea.

It will be appreciated that Stages 6 and 7 constitute very advanced work. It should also be realised that the task of weight-bearing on the hands can be used in other phases of the lesson:

(a) in the Introductory phase;
(b) in the Class Activity phase;
(c) as a task in Group Work;
(d) as a type of movement to be included in sequences, with or without apparatus, in either Part I or Part II of the lesson.

BALANCE

Balance is a most interesting and challenging task for children of all ages, and just as children have always enjoyed balancing on their hands, so also do they enjoy working on the idea of balancing on other parts of the body—feet, knees, hips, shoulders, elbows, head, etc. Balance requires control and implies taking, supporting or moving the body weight on one or more small parts of the body.

This task can be presented to the children on an *individual*, *partner* or *small group* basis, but teachers should appreciate that partner and group co-operation in this phase, as elsewhere in the lesson, is a development from work of an individual nature and that the children should be ready for this more advanced stage. How do we introduce and develop work on this idea? Throughout this book the educational value of individual exploration and invention has always been stressed and in this phase the application of this principle is equally important. Children should be allowed to discover the various ways of balancing for themselves rather than have a specific way imposed upon them. The teacher will therefore develop this theme on lines similar to the following:

1 (a) Show me a position of balance.
  (b) Can you hold this position?
  (c) Is it stretched or curled, etc.?
  (d) Is it really stretched or curled?
2 Find other ways of balancing.
  Here the teacher allows the children:
  (a) to *experiment* and to *explore* new ways for themselves;
  (b) to *watch* each other (Demonstration);
  (c) to *answer questions* put to them in relation to the task set (Question and answer technique);

29 Rolling—wide and stretched

30 'Twist as you move'

31 Positions of balance are possible on most equipment

32 Sequences based on bridging and arching

(*d*) to *comment* on the similarities and differences in the demonstrations seen (Observation).

Further exploration will then be influenced by the factors commented upon in (*d*) above, such as *body part, shape*, etc. The teacher can also draw the children's attention to those factors which influence their choice and experimentation, for this teaching technique, which is valuable in all phases of the work, not only produces new ideas but also increases the children's awareness and understanding.

E.g. (*a*) In your practice think about the *part* or *parts of the body*
on which you are balancing.
(*b*) Think about your *body shape* as you balance.
(*c*) How *many parts* of your body are you balancing on?
(*d*) Is your balance *still* or *moving*? etc.

Another very successful method of development is to *relate the main task*, i.e. Balance, *to other factors*.

E.g. (*a*) Find ways of balancing on your hands, shoulders, feet,
etc. (*Body part.*)
(*b*) Find ways of balancing on three parts, two parts of
your body, etc. (*Number of parts.*)
(*c*) Find ways of balancing in stretched, wide, symmetrical
positions, etc. (*Shape.*)
(*d*) Find ways of balancing with your body inverted.
(*Space.*) (See Plate 27.)

Having given the children the opportunity to experiment and to experience different ways of balancing and having developed confidence and ability as well as understanding, the children will now be ready to:

3 Combine different ways of balancing and
4 Produce sequences based on this task, often using other kinds of
movements, e.g. rolling, to make their sequences flow more
smoothly.

It is also advisable to allow the children further opportunities for experimentation and it will be found that the new and often more advanced ideas will frequently replace or supplement those produced in the earlier phases of experimentation (Stage 2). In addition the children can be challenged to include some positions of balance in sequences based on a combination of different types of movements.

Balance can also be incorporated most successfully in group work, where it is possible through the use of large apparatus to present interesting and challenging situations conducive to individual balance and subsequently to partner and group practices based on this idea (see Plates 28 and 41).

CLASS ACTIVITIES (see Chapters 5-7, 9, 10)

So much apparatus is used in the earlier part of the lesson that there is now far less need for class activities based on the old idea of appropriate preparation for group work. However, we include in Part I a section which, if the teacher wishes, may be devoted to class activities. This could take the form of:

(a) Practice with a particular kind of apparatus, e.g. blocks, blocks and canes, hoops, ropes, etc.

(b) Practice of particular types of movements which might require special attention and additional practice, e.g. jumping and landing, work on the hands, rolling, etc.

(c) Practice of specific activities or features in which the children display special interest, e.g. hand-stand, leap-frog, balance, etc.

(d) Different aspects of partner co-operation (see p. 188 and Plates 33 and 34).

Relaxation

The ability to relax is essential to all good movement, but not all children possess this ability and they may have to be taught how to relax. Tenseness is wasteful of effort and detrimental to good performance, so that, in addition to specific practice of relaxation, the principles of controlled relaxation must be applied. The ability to relax completely while lying on the floor is only part of the training required; the children must also learn to relax effectively while performing their various activities. In the early stages it is necessary to know and feel the difference between being tense and being loose, so that later the child not only can consciously relax but, when necessary, will do so involuntarily.

No special place in the lesson is suggested for this training but the teacher should introduce it incidentally as and when the need arises. Stiffness, awkwardness and general below-standard work are usually signs of the need to introduce more training and practice in relaxation; conversely the need for special relaxation training will diminish as the ability of the class improves.

Training in relaxation should be done indoors, unless the weather is exceptionally good.

Teaching method

There is a place here, especially in the early stages of relaxation training, for rather more direct teaching than in most of the Primary School Physical Education lesson. Perhaps the reason is that this is a particular skill which has to be taught rather than an activity which could be evolved by experiment and invention. Thus the early stages of such training might follow these lines:

'Sit down and let me see you shaking your hands loosely,' followed by such comments as, 'Shake all the water off!' etc.
'Now make your hands tight and hard like icicles and try to shake them.'

The difference will quickly be noticed and should be discussed. The children can then practise these activities freely, and try out the same ideas with other parts of the body, e.g. the foot, leg, shoulder, head; or while the body is in different positions, e.g. lying down, standing or kneeling. Having learned the difference between being loose or relaxed and tight or tense the children can now freely practise relaxation with various parts of the body. The important and ultimate aim is to ensure that the children develop the ability to use their bodies economically and fluently.

Posture

Modern work in Physical Education has frequently been criticised because of an apparent lack of attention to the important matter of posture. There is no doubt that if, as a result of a change of approach in our teaching, the posture of children has deteriorated, then this criticism, by School Medical Officers and others, is justified, for good posture is of vital importance.

Children should be trained to adopt good positions in sitting, standing, walking and running, and although many do this naturally, others need frequent correction and constant reminders of what is required. Attention to posture should be given informally from the earliest stages, but if posture training is to be really effective the children should understand the purpose and aim of the training, and appreciate its full value and its contribution to good health and complete physical development. Through demonstration and observation the children should be trained to recognise the important features of good posture and should be encouraged to apply this knowledge and understanding to their own needs. Teachers may occasionally require to give more direct guidance to the children in this matter. It is therefore necessary for them to understand what is meant by good posture and to develop the ability to recognise faults and defects. Minor faults of posture should be corrected informally at all times, but cases of bad posture resulting from physical defects should be dealt with individually in special posture or remedial classes, or if necessary should be referred to the school clinic.

Training in good posture is a responsibility of all teachers at all times, but during Physical Education lessons, when the children are properly changed, the teacher can more easily detect any faults or deformities which might be present.

'The child with the flat chest, round shoulders, poking head and prominent abdomen may be the rule rather than the exception and in such a case we often find some degree of spinal curvature, flat feet or a reduced expansion of the base of the chest. It is just because these defects are so common, because they are hidden by the clothes, and because the teacher's eye is so accustomed to a poor carriage that there is often a complete failure to realise how extremely bad is the average posture of the class. Obviously, deformities or marked departures from the normal are easy to detect, but these cases belong rather to the clinic than to the school. It is the incipient and minor defects, just those which the ordinary class work should help to prevent or remove, which are not so easy to discover. The aim should be, above all, to prevent defects.' (*Syllabus of Physical Training for Schools*, 1933.)

Good posture is maintained with the least possible strain on the muscles and tissues which hold the bones and joints in their proper places. The body is supported equally by both feet with the feet almost straight forward. The knees are straight but not hyper-extended and the pelvis tilted just sufficiently to maintain the normal forward curve of the lumbar spine. Excessive tilting of the pelvic girdle in either a forward or backward direction will produce faulty positions. The normal curvature of the spine should be maintained and exaggerated curves which cause hollow back, round back, or poking head should be avoided.

FIG. 13

Reaching up with the top of the head, 'growing tall', and other similar suggestions will help to correct and improve poor positions. The isolated instruction, 'Keep your shoulders back', is incorrect and often results in strained effort. The arms should hang loosely with the shoulders relaxed but not dropping forward, the back of the neck should be straight and the chin drawn in just sufficiently to avoid a poking head. In a good position tenseness and rigidity are eliminated, the maximum effect being obtained with the minimum of effort (see Fig. 13).

Home environment, nutrition, suitable clothing, footwear, and adequate rest all influence the general poise, carriage and deportment of children; bad posture may often be a reflection of emotional strain, mental attitude, and lack of pride or confidence. Nevertheless the contribution of the school staff, together with regular participation in Physical Education, is of paramount importance in the development and maintenance of good posture.

CHAPTER 8

Group Work

Aims

As soon as possible, even at the Infant stage, children should be trained to work in small groups. One of the main problems is that of organisation and we feel it would be valuable to give some attention to the details of this important aspect of group work.

The value of this part of the lesson is based not merely on the necessity for organisation into small groups which move in turn to use apparatus which is supplied in limited quantities, but much more on the positive contribution made by training the children to work together in small groups, often isolated from the direct control and supervision of the teacher. The social value of this training, together with training in handling and moving the apparatus, in taking care of it and in using it to the fullest extent, cannot be over-emphasised.

It cannot be denied that the time required to conform to the set pattern of 'free standing' exercises in Part I of the 1933 Syllabus lesson made it difficult for the teacher to allow enough time to make the fullest use of the second part of the lesson. Now that the teacher is allowed much more freedom to plan the lesson, which has itself been allocated more time, group work is usually given an adequate proportion of the time available.

The experiences enjoyed and the skill developed in the first part of the lesson should be applied to the new situations met in the various groups. The work is assessed by the way the children perform as members of the group, by the standard of performance reached by each individual child, by how much the children can do on their own, by the children's understanding of the ways in which they move, and by their ability to use the various parts of their bodies efficiently and imaginatively in all situations. This carry-over from the first to the second part of the lesson is very evident in all good work and is of the greatest importance.

Organisation

There are many ways in which group work can be introduced in the early stages. One way is to allow the children to work in two groups and later to divide into four groups, ensuring all the time that there is a piece of small apparatus for each child, e.g. small mats, skipping ropes, hoops and small balls, etc.

To illustrate this development, we give a diagrammatic representation of the progression from one to four groups.

Stage I The class practises in one group with one piece of small apparatus for each child.

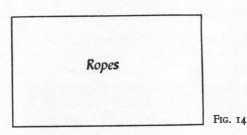

Ropes

Fig. 14

By using this method, but changing the apparatus used, the children become familiar with several pieces of small apparatus, e.g. small balls, wooden blocks, skipping ropes, individual mats, hoops, etc.

Stage II The class practises in two groups, each group using a different kind of small apparatus.

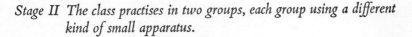

Ropes | Blocks

Fig. 15

The apparatus may be changed until the children have had experience and training in the use of at least four kinds of small apparatus.

Stage III The class practises in four groups with four types of small apparatus.

Small balls	Ropes
Blocks	Mats

FIG. 16

The children can now be taught to move round from group to group and it is advisable to teach the use of 'group places'. A certain amount of formality in the early stages of changing from group to group is essential, but ultimately the children should be capable of moving from one group to the next with the minimum of formality. It must be remembered that informal changing from group to group does not mean chaos or noise and rushing wildly from one piece of apparatus to the next.

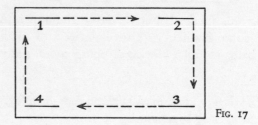

FIG. 17

The following suggestions for training the children to change from group to group will be found useful, each step being determined by the ability and progress of the class.

1 'Run to group places—begin working—stop—return to the same group place—run and stand in the NEXT group place—start work.' It is often helpful with very young children to ask them to point to the next group place before they move

to it. All this movement is controlled by the teacher to ensure that they all arrive at the right place at the right time.

2 'Run to group places—begin working—stop—run to the next group place—start work.' This movement is still controlled by the teacher, but eliminates the necessity of the children returning to the group place associated with the apparatus they have just been using, with a consequent saving of time.

3 'Run to group places—begin working—stop—move to the next place and start working immediately.'

4 'Run to group places—begin working—change to the next group and start working immediately.'

The children must be trained to place the apparatus they have been using quietly and neatly on the ground, or, in the case of balls, into the containers provided, to prevent them rolling away. When the children have been trained as suggested above, the teacher should vary the method of changing so that the children do not take any one method for granted.

In a very short time the children should be capable of working in smaller groups and, in fact, when large apparatus is introduced into group work the class should be divided into groups of not more than four or five children. Some teachers have found that the change from four to eight groups is often too difficult, particularly for younger children, if made at the same time as a change of apparatus. It is suggested therefore that an interim stage can be introduced with advantage. This involves retaining the same apparatus as in Stage III but dividing the class into eight groups instead of four.

Stage IV The class practises in eight groups with the same four pieces of apparatus as in Stage III.

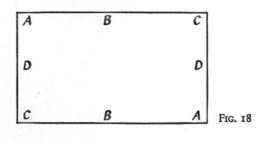

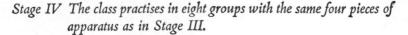

FIG. 18

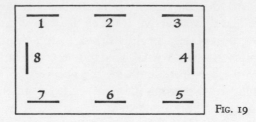

FIG. 19

A, B, C and D represent the four types of apparatus.

The group places are indicated in Fig. 19.

It will be seen that groups 1 and 5 will be using the same type of apparatus, as also will groups 2 and 6, 3 and 7, 4 and 8.

If this scheme is followed, it should now be possible to introduce at least one piece of large apparatus in place of the small apparatus used by that group. The group using this large apparatus would at first be under the direct supervision of the teacher, for it is reasonable to assume that the other groups of children are able to carry on working independently with the now familiar pieces of small apparatus.

Stage V The class practises in eight groups, one group using large apparatus.

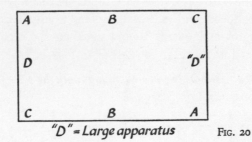

"D" = Large apparatus   FIG. 20

Further items of large apparatus and different kinds of small apparatus may now be introduced one by one, until ultimately the children work in eight groups and each group activity is different from the rest.

Stage VI The class practises in eight groups with eight different types of apparatus (including large apparatus).

It will not always be possible for all groups to be working on large apparatus. If, for example, only four pieces of large apparatus are available it is recommended that these be dispersed so that groups use small and large apparatus alternately.

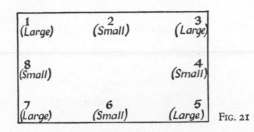

FIG. 21

E.g. Group 1 Large apparatus (climbing frame)
Group 2 Small apparatus (small balls)
Group 3 Large apparatus (wooden jumping boxes and large mats)
Group 4 Small apparatus (individual mats)
Group 5 Large apparatus (climbing frame)
Group 6 Small apparatus (skipping ropes)
Group 7 Large apparatus (benches and large mats)
Group 8 Small apparatus (2, 3 or 4 blocks and canes)

This arrangement, and the organisation and planning of group work generally, depends upon the amount and type of large apparatus available. The teacher should site large apparatus in order to ensure that apparatus of the same type, e.g. climbing apparatus, is so dispersed that climbing and heaving are not demanded of the children in successive groups. (See examples below.)

E.g. Group 1 Parallel ropes
Group 2 Benches for balance work
Group 3 Window ladder unit
Group 4 Boxes for jumping from a height
Group 5 Portable climbing unit
Group 6 Junior vaulting box, etc.
Group 7 Pole and tripod stands
Group 8 Inclined bench and trestle with large mats

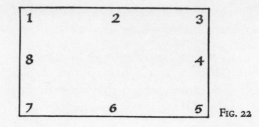

FIG. 22

For simplification and efficiency we strongly recommend the use of 'perimeter' positions for group places, as indicated in Figs. 21 and 22. In this way changing from group to group in either direction, clockwise or anti-clockwise, is facilitated, and the method of organisation is easily understood and followed by the children.

Siting equipment

It is recommended that the larger portable apparatus should be used as near as possible to the place where it is normally kept. It follows from this that, if possible, the large portable apparatus should be dispersed round the hall when not in use. This is not always practicable, particularly in schools with limited facilities, so that some thought will have to be given, when planning group work, to the arrangement of the apparatus in order to avoid taking up too much time carrying the apparatus about the hall. There are other factors which influence the siting of equipment and these should also be given careful consideration, for example:

1 Keep the apparatus away from doors, radiators, windows, etc., and especially avoid having children landing near or in the direction of such obstructions.
2 Arrange the apparatus so that children do not congregate in any one place, e.g. different groups should not start, or finish, at the same place.
3 Use all available space, and site the apparatus to allow floor space to be used in conjunction with it whenever this is possible.

124

4 Position ball practices, if included, in a corner and as much out of the way as possible, so that interference with other groups, especially with jumping groups, is avoided.

5 Avoid jumping towards the windows (and light)—'Jump into the hall—not the wall!'

6 Combine several pieces of apparatus in each group whenever possible, to present the children with interesting and challenging situations.

To summarise, the siting should be planned in order to achieve:

(a) maximum use of the space available;
(b) maximum use of the apparatus available;
(c) maximum activity;
(d) maximum variety;
and (e) maximum safety.

This is accomplished by careful planning and preparation (Fig. 23).

Storage of large apparatus

Consideration must be given to the problem of finding the best places for large apparatus to be stored when not in use. Each school has its own problems and peculiarities in this respect, but, generally speaking, dispersal of large apparatus is better than concentration in one section of the hall. Permanent positions indicated by marks or lines on the floor are a great help.

Where space is extremely limited certain items of large apparatus might be in the open spaces under climbing frames, etc., as shown in Plate 36.

Group places

It is essential that the children know their group places and it is recommended that at the commencement of 'group work' the children should first run to their group places. The advantages of starting in this way are as follows:

1 It helps to establish control and discipline.
2 It provides an opportunity for the teacher to check the number

Primary school hall (50ft x 30ft)

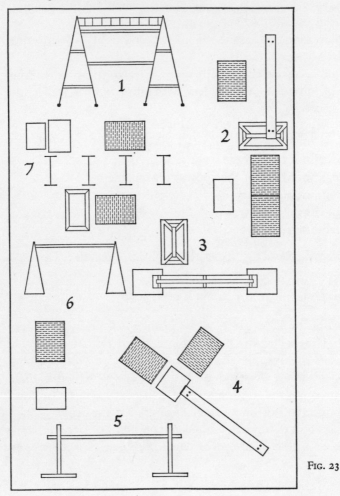

FIG. 23

group	apparatus	group	apparatus

1 Climbing frame: two trestles (7ft), one ladder (9ft), one bar (9ft), one bar (6ft 7in.).

2 Inclined bench on trestle (2ft 4in.), three mats (4ft × 3ft), one jumping box (2ft).

3 Inverted bench on slotted jumping boxes (2ft), trestle (2ft 4in.).

4 Inclined bench on vaulting stool (3ft 6in.), two mats (4ft × 3ft).

5 Two cup-shaped stands (3ft 3in.), one wooden pole (14ft).

6 One jumping box (2ft), one mat 4ft × 3ft, two metal trestles (4ft), one bar (9ft).

7a One bar box, one mat (4ft × 3ft); skittles and canes—common to a and b; one jumping box (1ft), one jumping box (2ft), one mat (4ft × 3ft)—b.

of children in each group, and if necessary to make any adjustments.

3 It enables the teacher to organise a change of apparatus or activity and to inform the whole class of this change without waste of time.

4 It gives the teacher a chance to make general comments about the group work or about the particular task to be set in any one group.

5 It allows the teacher to move the children either clockwise or anti-clockwise from group to group, or, if necessary, to begin at the group next to the one at which they finished in the previous lesson. It is not always possible for the children to work at all the groups every lesson, so the teacher must organise his group work with this in mind.

It should be the aim of all teachers to train the children to put away whatever apparatus they happen to be using at the end of the lesson, but, in the early stages, it is recommended that the children should return to their *own* group place, and put away the apparatus which they got out originally. This method has proved the most effective.

Team leaders

The appointment of team leaders has previously been a feature of group work, but we are very doubtful if there is any real justification for a continuation of this system. Small groups are able to work quite successfully without being ordered about and organised by a leader, and it seems more valuable to leave each child free to use his initiative and for powers of leadership to emerge from the opportunities provided for working as a member of a small group. All children should take an equal share in the responsibilities for moving apparatus and taking care of the equipment used.

Formation of groups

1 New groups should not be formed each lesson; this is both unnecessary and a waste of time. It should only be necessary to make minor changes occasionally.

2 Groups can successfully be formed in several ways, but we favour a method which allows the children to form themselves into their own groups containing the required number of children. In this way we might find groups of similar ability, of the same sex, or mixed.
3 Frequent changing of children between groups should be avoided—a degree of permanency is advisable.
4 In classes which have a very wide age range, for example in small or rural schools, it will probably be necessary to ensure that each group is composed of children of approximately the same age to enable them to work more successfully together as a group in relation to the apparatus provided.

Number of groups

The number of groups in a class depends on the number of children in the class and the amount of apparatus available. Though we have previously illustrated our remarks on group work by reference to eight groups, this should not be taken as a rule to be followed with all classes. Most types of large apparatus make it unwise to have more than four or five children in any one group. If no large apparatus is available the number of children in each group is not so important, provided that each child is actively occupied and as much variety as possible has been planned from group to group.

Time allocation

1 As a general rule, approximately half the lesson should be available for group work and if possible group work should be a part of every lesson. There are some schools where and some occasions when this is not practicable, e.g. where the lessons are very short or where the apparatus is difficult to get out or to erect, etc. It is recommended that in these circumstances the teacher should devote a whole lesson to Part I and the next lesson to group work. If this is done, the children should take part in a vigorous activity before beginning group work.

33 Partner bridging

34 'Support your partner's body weight'

35 Three types of climbing equipment erected in a small Infant School hall

36 Each school can solve its own storage problems

37 Working individually

38 Co-operating as a group—the movement selected by the children

39 'How many ways of hanging can you find?'

40 The task—'inverted wide shapes'

2 Many teachers do not allow the children to spend enough time at each group to make the practice worth while; in their anxiety to allow the children an opportunity to work with all the apparatus, they move the children from group to group too frequently. If it is not possible for the children to work at all the groups in any one lesson, the teacher must ensure in the next lesson that they have an opportunity to work with the apparatus missed in the previous lesson. Alternatively the teacher can move the children from group to group in a clockwise direction in one lesson, and in an anticlockwise direction in the next.

An able and experienced class could with advantage spend more than half the lesson on group work. But we emphasise our firm belief that really successful group work, in terms of ability of the class and the ideas they express, is closely related to and richly influenced by the work done in the first part of the lesson.

Continuity

It is unnecessary for the teacher to describe the apparatus to be used and the work to be done by the various groups in every lesson. Group work should follow on from the previous lesson and the teacher should be able to say, 'Get out the apparatus for group work and begin working!' without any further preliminaries. Minor modifications to the arrangement of apparatus, or to the task set for one or more of the groups, should be made during the lesson so that at the end of the lesson the group work will usually be the same as that which begins the group work in the next lesson. Thus the work is developed and the teacher ensures that there is continuity and that changes are made gradually.

Sub-division of a group

Where it is possible to include more than one piece of the same type of large apparatus in any one group, e.g. large mats, benches, etc., it is recommended that the children at these groups be further divided into smaller groups. This reduces the necessity to queue for turns, increases the amount of activity and occasionally makes it possible to present more than one type of task in the one group. It also avoids giving the children the feeling they are being chased round by four or five children behind them. Two sub-groups (Fig. 24) are better than one group (Fig. 25).

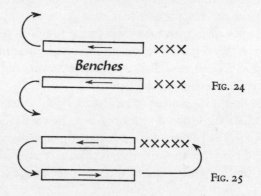

Benches

Fig. 24

Fig. 25

The children should be encouraged to use the space available on the way back to their starting place, and this can be varied by the use of additional small apparatus, e.g. hoops, blocks, blocks and canes, mats, etc.

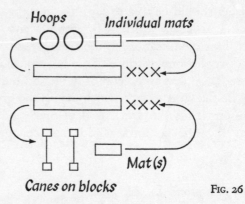

Hoops   *Individual mats*

Canes on blocks   *Mat(s)*

Fig. 26

Variety of apparatus within a group

In dealing with Part I of the lesson we have frequently referred to the presentation of opportunities for children to combine movements and activities in sequences or patterns. In much the same way it is possible for children to do this in group work by using different kinds of apparatus in the same group. The children make sequences incorporating the apparatus provided, together with any additional floor space which is available (Fig. 27).

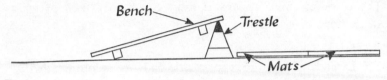

FIG. 27

A further step can sometimes be recommended—to allow the children to arrange the apparatus at their disposal according to their own ideas. This stage should be reached only when the children are familiar with the apparatus and have had ample opportunity to explore its possibilities. Much ingenuity will be used, and co-operation between children in arranging the apparatus wisely has educational value; but the teacher must ensure that all the time available is not being used in rearranging and moving the apparatus so that the children never really make use of it.

The content of group work

We have already said that large apparatus should be introduced as soon as possible into group work and that small apparatus should only be used if there is not sufficient large apparatus available. Teachers are reminded that when it is necessary to use both small and large apparatus in group work, the work should be planned so that the children use small and large apparatus alternately.

The content of group work will depend among other things on:

1 the amount of space available;
2 the amount and type of apparatus available;
3 the number and age of the children in the class;

131

4 the ability and needs of the class;
5 the need to provide variety;
and 6 whether the lesson is to be indoors or out of doors.

Use of small apparatus

The types of small apparatus most commonly used in group work are:

> Small balls;
> Large balls (5-in. to 8-in. plastic balls are recommended);
> Playbats and gamester balls;
> Hoops;
> Wooden blocks;
> Individual rubber mats;
> Skipping ropes;
> Vaulting poles with rubber ferrules;
> Skittles and canes.

Use of large balls

Large ball practices can be carried out individually, with a partner, or in small groups, and the following are suitable practices—there are of course many others. For obvious reasons, most of these practices are more suited to outdoor lessons, where space is not so limited.

INDIVIDUAL PRACTICES

1 Throwing and catching (occasionally against a wall).
2 Throwing and catching on the move.
3 Bouncing practices:
  (a) on the move,
  (b) in various directions,
  (c) changing directions,
  (d) with variation of speed, etc.
4 Dribbling practices with the feet (inside, outside, etc., as in soccer).
5 Heading practices.

132

6 Practices against a wall:

e.g. (*a*) heading,
    (*b*) trapping (soccer),
    (*c*) throwing (soccer, rugby, netball),
    (*d*) passing,
    (*e*) kicking,
    (*f*) 'keeping the ball up'—with or without a wall.

PRACTICES IN PAIRS

1 Throwing and catching (stationary). This will at first be free practice, though from time to time the children's attention should be drawn to the following variations:

(*a*) under-arm throw,
(*b*) two-handed chest throw,
(*c*) one-handed chest throw,
(*d*) Rugby passing,
(*e*) overhead throw (soccer).

2 Throwing and catching on the move.
3 Soccer practices.
4 Netball practices.
5 Practices against a wall.

SMALL GROUP PRACTICES

1 Game-like practices and small team games:
   e.g. (*a*) team passing (hand or foot);
       (*b*) consecutive team passing (2 v 2; 3 v 3; etc.).
2 All the practices given for individuals and pairs, but adapted for use with three, four or five children.
3 Groups should sometimes be given the opportunity to make up their own games.

Large apparatus

As we noted in Chapter 1, one of the most important developments in Primary School Physical Education of recent years has been the introduction of large apparatus and the much greater use of such equipment by all children of Primary School age. The need to provide opportunity for Primary School children to climb, hang and heave—all natural activities—was very apparent and a large variety of different types of climbing equipment can now be seen in most Primary Schools. Though the types vary, and include scrambling nets, heaving bars, climbing frames, climbing ropes, parallel ropes, jungle gyms, etc., they all satisfy the same basic needs. In addition to climbing apparatus there are various pieces of equipment available to provide opportunities for jumping, balancing, vaulting and activities of a general agility character. This equipment includes vaulting boxes, small and large wooden boxes, trestles and stands of various kinds on which benches and planks can be placed. Thus it is now possible to familiarise Primary School children with large portable and fixed apparatus on which they can exercise their imagination, inventiveness and powers of exploration, and enjoy the thrill, excitement and pleasure which experience on such equipment will provide.

We have already referred (p. 123) to the advantages of dispersing large items of equipment, especially those which present a similar challenge, e.g. climbing apparatus. Also, to avoid a concentration of children at any one point, we prefer to see several single units, each accommodating one group of four or five children, rather than a large unit which contains many sections, occupies a great deal of space and has to accommodate many groups of children in the same place and at the same time.

Suggestions for the use of large apparatus in group work

1 Before the equipment is used, the teacher should ensure that it is safe, that it is fixed securely and that it is not in need of repair. Arrangements for the regular inspection of the apparatus, both portable and fixed, will normally be made by the local authority to ensure that the apparatus is in good condition. The teacher should immediately take out of use any equipment about which there is any doubt.

2 Not more than four or five children should be allowed on a piece of apparatus at any one time, so that all are able to occupy themselves safely and actively. The aim should be to be found 'working' not 'waiting'.

3 Children must be trained to make use of all parts of the apparatus where this is applicable, e.g. on a climbing frame they should use the ends and the lower parts of the equipment as well as the middle and top parts which are often the more attractive. In this way, congestion will be avoided and much greater variety of movement will be developed by each child.
4 Large apparatus should be used only during the lesson and under the supervision of the teacher in order to avoid its misuse and possible damage.
5 It should be part of the children's duty to assemble and, if necessary, erect this apparatus, and specific training may have to be given to ensure that this is done with safety and efficiency.
6 In schools where such equipment is not readily accessible or easily erected, it is often a good idea to erect the equipment at the beginning of the day and to leave it up for several classes to use before taking it down at the end of the day or session.

Teaching method with large apparatus

We are quite certain that the Indirect teaching method described in previous chapters is the correct one to use when children are first introduced to large apparatus. This method allows the children to have a completely free choice of activity, limited only by the nature of the apparatus being used. The safety and confidence of the children is ensured by the precautions taken by the teacher in seeing that the equipment is safe to use and that the children work quietly so that difficulties of supervision are minimised.

How long should children be left free to explore and experiement?

This is a common query and the answer is important.

There is a primary need for all children to be allowed to gain confidence in using large apparatus. This confidence results most easily and effectively from the opportunities allowed to the children in the early stages to experiment freely, to find out what they can do, to become acquainted with the apparatus, and to learn and to develop at their own rate and in their own time. Thus each gains in confidence because the teacher avoids the mistake of asking the child to attempt prescribed activities or movements which may be either too simple or too difficult.

It is our experience that children unconsciously refrain from attempting anything that is beyond their power.

The time allowed for exploration and discovery should be longer with younger children, but at all ages there is a need for some opportunity for this to be given. Usually teachers tend to allow this period of completely free experimentation to last too long with the result that practice becomes purposeless and the children spend their time repeating the same few things lesson after lesson. The aim is for each child to produce the maximum variety of which he or she is capable, and therefore the teacher should, as soon as possible, introduce some measure of limitation, however small, to ensure a definite and positive effort on the part of the child. Examples suitable for this part of the training will be given later, in respect of particular pieces of apparatus, but the first stage should be to let the children in the class see the different ways in which the apparatus is being used so that each may, if so inclined, make use of the ideas presented to him. Over a series of lessons, each group should have an opportunity to show what it can do at each piece of apparatus.

The teacher's chief difficulty is to know what sort of limitation to set.

He can:

1 Impose a task common to all groups;
2 Impose a different task in each group;
3 Impose a task in some groups while others are allowed to work and choose quite freely.

In the early stages this limitation should be of a general nature.

E.g. *Using the benches*
    (*a*) What can you do *along* the bench?
    (*b*) What can you do *over* the bench?

Using the climbing frame
    (*a*) Find ways of moving *along* the bar.
    (*b*) Find ways of moving *up* and *down* the apparatus.

Later, tasks of a more specific nature can be set so that the demands made increase the difficulty.

E.g. *Using the benches*
    (*a*) What kind of jumping can you do along or off the bench?
    (*b*) Find ways of moving along the bench on your hands and your feet.

    Using the climbing frame
    (*a*) Find ways of moving along the bar, stretching your body as much as possible.
    (*b*) How many ways of hanging from the apparatus can you find?

Limitations or tasks can be related to:

1 A *type of movement*, e.g. jumping, rolling, balancing, stretching and curling, twisting, hanging, etc.

2 The *prepositional* use of apparatus, e.g. over, off, round, along, under, against, between, etc.

3 The *part of the body* to be used;
    e.g. (*a*) From how many different parts of the body can you hang?
    (*b*) Go over the apparatus making your feet the highest part of your body.
    (*c*) Leave the apparatus from your hands.

4 The *shape of the body* during the movement;
    e.g. (*a*) Make your body stretch and curl on the apparatus.
    (*b*) Concentrate on wide shapes in your sequence over and round the apparatus.

5 The direction factor;
    e.g. (*a*) Think about the direction of your movement.
    (*b*) Leave the apparatus in different directions.
    (*c*) Can you change direction as you move over or along your apparatus?
    (*d*) Devise a sequence on your apparatus showing frequent changes of direction.

6 The *speed* factor;

e.g. (*a*) Select a movement on the apparatus and endeavour to practise it at different speeds.

(*b*) Try to include a quick and slow movement in your practice.

7 The *space* factor;

e.g. (*a*) Use your body on the apparatus as high as you can.

(*b*) Show both a static (still) and mobile (moving) balance.

8 *Combinations* of the above limitations;

e.g. (*a*) Move *over* the apparatus making your body *stretch and curl*.

(*b*) Practise *rolling* (mats or bars) showing variation in *speed, shape* or *direction*.

When an idea or task has been given to the class, sufficient time must be allowed for the children to work out their answers, and in most cases several lessons should be devoted to this. Children should be selected for demonstration purposes to illustrate the many different ways in which the particular problem has been solved, and all should be encouraged not only to see the many differences for themselves but also to try out as many of the ideas expressed as possible. This does not necessarily mean that they should practise exactly what they have seen, but that they should use the ideas to help them in their own exploration.

Time must then be allowed for repetition and consolidation and for improvement in performance before proceeding to another idea or task. To have solved a problem is one thing, to execute a movement or activity well is another. This demands practice, concentration, perseverance and understanding by the child as well as good coaching by the teacher.

It will be seen that though we have recommended the use of the Indirect and the Limitation Methods, we have not suggested the use of the Direct teaching method when using large apparatus in group work. This is deliberate. Except when a child desires to learn a specific movement and requests help from the teacher, we consider that the use of the Direct Method is not advisable when using large apparatus, but that some measure of choice should always be given. This allows the children to progress at their own rate and is the most valuable safety precaution possible. Experience has shown that in spite of the introduction of this type of apparatus and of the exciting and sometimes advanced work done by some of the children, accidents have been virtually nil, and this, we are sure, is the result of the teaching methods employed.

Group work provides the opportunity for applying all that the children have learnt in the earlier part of the lesson. The tasks set, and the ability of the children to solve them, will reflect the effectiveness of the previous teaching. If children are asked, for example, to show how many ways they can jump from the apparatus, or stretch and curl on the climbing frame, their variety and skill will depend to a great extent on the effectiveness of their previous training.

Types of large apparatus

Generally speaking, large apparatus provides activities of three main types:

1 Climbing, hanging and heaving;
2 Jumping;
3 General agility, including balance, rolling, etc.

Equipment for climbing, hanging and heaving

Some types of climbing equipment are very elaborate and expensive; they also present certain difficulties, such as those of erection and storage, and of the concentration of many children in one confined space. A less elaborate type of equipment is preferred which does not take up so much space, which can easily be erected and stored, but which will occupy a maximum of five children effectively and safely at any one time. There are numerous examples of this type of equipment and some Education Authorities have shown a preference for particular items or have designed their own apparatus. Some of these items are fixed (see Plate 35); others which are portable have the advantage of being available for both outdoor and indoor use. All are very effective and greatly appreciated by the children, who benefit from the experience afforded them.

Among the types of apparatus recommended are:

1 *Climbing ropes*

These should, whenever possible, be fixed on a sliding track which enables them to be brought easily and quickly into use and effectively stored away afterwards. They take up very little floor space when in use and practically none at all when not in use. These are important factors.

Use of climbing ropes

The principle of 'free choice' must be applied when using climbing ropes. The children must at first be left free to climb—and to find out how to climb. Each child should develop his own technique, and coaching by the teacher will consist of demonstrations by different children and discussions with the class regarding aspects of individual variations. In this way the children will become familiar with the apparatus and confident in using it; the only direct instruction necessary at this stage is concerned with coming down and not with going up the ropes. The children must be told NOT to slide down the rope—if they do so they are likely to burn their hands, which can be both painful and extremely harmful.

The variety produced by the children will result from exploration and from observation of each other. Though pleasing progress will be made, further improvement in their versatility, adaptability and skill will only result from stimulation by the teacher, or by the imposition of some limitation in the way the apparatus is used.

E.g. 1 How many different ways can you climb the rope?
    2 What can you do between two ropes?
    3 Can you climb two ropes?
    4 What kind of positions can you adopt, or what kind of shapes can you make, on the rope?
    5 How many different ways can you hang from the rope?
    6 Can you climb from one rope to another?

7 Can you stretch and curl your body on the ropes?
8 Can you twist your body on one or two ropes?

Both teachers and children will find great interest in seeing the many different ways in which these problems can be solved. The use of demonstration, observation and questioning is important and will not only help in increasing the repertoire of each individual child, but also in enabling each child to solve in several ways the problem set.

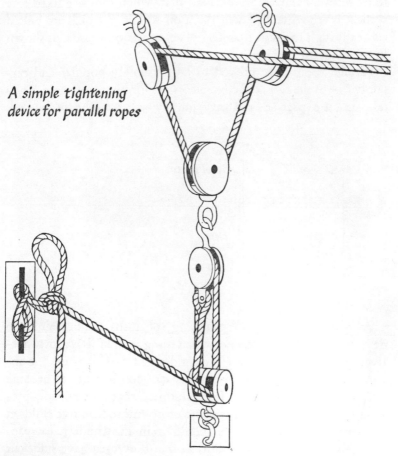

A simple tightening device for parallel ropes

FIG. 28

2 Parallel ropes

These consist of two ropes about 18 to 20 inches apart, fixed horizontally or inclined at heights of 5 feet 6 inches to 6 feet 6 inches, depending on the children's ages. They are tightened by a block and tackle (see Fig. 28) or other tensioning device, and can be fixed either across a hall, across a corner of a hall, or outside on stands fixed in concrete.

The span should not exceed 24 feet and ought not to be less than about 16 feet to be really effective. It is essential that they are fixed securely and we have found that, when they are fixed to a wall, it is advisable to fasten them on to hooks which are bolted right through the wall to a steel plate on the other side, as shown in the diagram (Fig. 29).

Parallel ropes have proved to be extremely popular and certainly one of the most effective pieces of climbing apparatus. They take up little space and can very quickly be erected or dismantled.

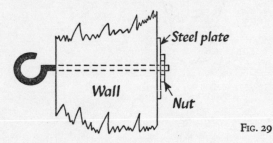

FIG. 29

Use of parallel ropes

As with all types of large climbing apparatus, the first aim is to develop the child's confidence when using it and this is most effectively achieved by allowing the children first of all to use the apparatus freely, to find out what they can do on it and to become familiar with the feel of it. It is presumed that the principle previously explained of having groups of not more than five children has been accepted. Teachers should train the children to space themselves out on the apparatus so that they each have sufficient space to work and move satisfactorily. The idea of queueing up for turns should be discouraged and the children should work wherever there is a space. It is helpful to put a chair at one end or a bench in the centre to enable smaller children to reach the rope.

The sequence followed by the teacher when this kind of apparatus is used should be:

1 Free practice and free choice;
2 Demonstration, observation and teacher stimulation;
3 Limiting the children to types of movements, activities or tasks;
4 Demonstration and observation of the ways the problems set have been solved;
5 Free practice: further exploration, observation and development.

Some suggested tasks when using parallel ropes

1 What can you do (*a*) under the ropes?
      (*b*) on top of the ropes?
      (*c*) round the ropes?
      (*d*) between the ropes?
      (*e*) along the ropes?
2 Can you make different shapes on the ropes?
3 (*a*) Can you stretch and curl on the ropes?
 (*b*) How many different ways can you stretch and curl?
4 Can you twist your body (*a*) on the ropes?
        (*b*) along or between the ropes?
How many different ways can you twist on the ropes?
5 How many bridge-like shapes can you make on the ropes?
6 How many wide shapes can you make on the ropes?
7 (*a*) How many different ways can you hang from the ropes?
 (*b*) Can you change from one hanging position to another?

Many combinations of the above suggestions are possible to increase the variety of activity and movement, as examples 8–10 show.

8 Can you move along the ropes making different shapes with your body?
9 Can you move along the ropes twisting or stretching your body?
10 Devise a sequence of different movements on the ropes.

These suggestions for the use of climbing ropes and parallel ropes apply equally to all other types of fixed or portable climbing apparatus, which might include scrambling nets, window ladder units, horizontal bars and ladders on portable trestles, 'jungle gym' units, etc.

Each of these various types of apparatus will have its own particular features and will produce types of movements peculiar to it. To make the best use of this apparatus the teacher must:

(a) allow free practice and free choice;
(b) impose limitations similar to those already suggested;
(c) use the technique of demonstration and observation, discussion and stimulation;
(d) demand high standards of performance;

and (e) give praise and encouragement whenever possible.

With regard to demonstration and observation, it is not enough merely to let the children show what they are doing. The teacher must train the children to observe, by directing their attention to important features and asking them questions about what they have seen. It is necessary to develop in the children the ability to recognise particular aspects of a demonstration and to notice similarities or differences between one child and another. The teacher may invite comments on the movements demonstrated to ensure that the children really understand what is involved in the performance of the particular movement or movements shown.

Jumping equipment

The ability to jump well is fundamental to physical efficiency, whether in games, athletics, or gymnastics, and children love to jump, especially from a height. The training in jumping which we have described in Chapter 6 and elsewhere and which is given in the first part of the lesson, finds its application in the thrill of jumping on, over, or from the large apparatus used in group work, and as in all other parts of the lesson the teacher must aim to improve the quality or standard of performance, and to increase the variety and experience of each individual child.

41 Balance work appeals to the children

42 All working and well spaced out along the ropes

43 'Matching' movements with a partner

44 Partner work within the group

Types of jumping equipment
These consist of:
> benches (lengthwise or crosswise);
> inclined benches or planks on trestle stands;
> vaulting boxes (junior size) and vaulting stools;
> boxes of various shapes and sizes;
> tables, desks, etc. (improvised);
> jumping stands;
> canes on skittles, etc.

Whatever kind of jumping apparatus is being used, the teacher should first ensure that it is firm, stable and safe; this applies particularly when using any type of improvised apparatus.

As with other large apparatus used in group work, children must first be allowed to develop confidence in using it and this is best accomplished by allowing them to practise freely without any limitations whatsoever. If this freedom is permitted, some children will soon begin jumping over or from the apparatus and in due course the teacher can deliberately impose this limitation by asking all the children to practise jumping and landing.

E.g. (*a*) Show me how you can jump from the apparatus.
(*b*) How many different ways can you jump from the apparatus?

It is necessary to do more than this—the teacher must make a real effort to increase the versatility of each child by the use of suitable demonstrations, intelligent observation of the differences shown, and by stimulating and encouraging the production, improvement and development of a wide variety of jumping movements.

The sort of differences which the teacher should encourage the children to observe would be the following:

1 What kind of a shape did he make in the air?
2 Did he jump from one foot or both feet?
3 What use did he make of his arms in the air?
4 In what direction did he jump?
5 Did he change his direction?
6 Did he change his position or shape in the air?

By watching these demonstrations, by observing and appreciating the many differences which will have been shown, the children will endeavour to practise some or all of these different kinds of jumps, thus increasing their own individual repertoire. This individual variety can also be encouraged by imposing a further limitation on the choice to be made by the child, i.e. relating another factor to the main task.

E.g. 1(a) Show me that you can jump from one foot as well as from both feet.
 (b) Show me any jumping practices from one foot.
 (c) Show me any jumping practices from both feet.
 2(a) Practise jumping in different directions.
 (b) Practise any kind of forward, backward, or sideways jump.
 3 Show me how you can turn or twist in the air.
 4 What you can do with your arms (or legs) in the air?
 5(a) What kind of a shape can you make in the air?
 A long shape?
 A wide shape?
 A curled shape? etc.
 (b) Can you change your shape in the air?

Increased variety can also be encouraged by placing landing mats at the side of the apparatus as well as, or instead of, behind (as shown in Fig. 30).

In addition to variety it is essential for the teacher at the same time to demand improved quality, that is, a better standard of performance. The basic essentials of a high standard of jumping

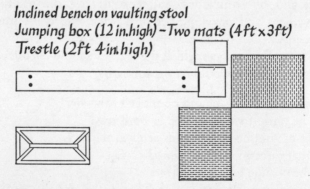

Inclined bench on vaulting stool
Jumping box (12 in. high) – Two mats (4ft x 3ft)
Trestle (2ft 4 in. high)

Fig. 30

146

are height, speed in take-off, stretch in the air (there are exceptions), lightness and resilience in take-off and landing, and control. These standards are obtained by practice, by repetition and consolidation, by the use of demonstrations, by intelligent observation, by effective coaching and encouragement, and by the teacher demanding the best effort of which each child is capable.

Having developed variety and encouraged quality in performance, jumping activities can successfully be linked with other activities and movements. (This may involve the use of additional apparatus, especially mats.) Children are capable of compiling sequences or patterns of their own. In these the jump may appear at the beginning, in the middle, or at the end.

> E.g. Using a sloping bench on a trestle with a mat beyond it, what can you do on, along or across the bench, how can you jump from the bench, and what can you do on or along the mat?

Further interest can be aroused by asking the children to work with a partner, evolving patterns or sequences which involve different aspects of partner co-operation.

Apparatus for general agility and balance

This heading includes all other types of apparatus which have not already been specially mentioned. There is much apparatus available for practice in agility and balance, and teachers and children can show great ingenuity in the arrangement of apparatus to increase interest and vary the situations facing the child.

Landing mats are often used for purposes other than landing, e.g. for rolling or for activities on the hands; they are also effective when used in combination with other apparatus to provide opportunities for sequences or patterns of movements, e.g. with wooden blocks, skittles and canes, hoops, jumping stands and so on. It is interesting to see the increased variety of movements produced when the mats are placed in different positions in relation to the other apparatus being used by the group.

Benches are used a great deal, and in many different ways. The following are some suggestions:

1 Free choice with benches lengthwise, crosswise, sloping or balance side uppermost.
2 With limitations such as:

   (a) along, across, on or from the bench;
   (b) using hands, feet, hands and feet, etc., on the bench;
   (c) heaving and pulling on the bench;
   (d) rolling or twisting on the bench;
   (e) using feet first, head first, etc., along the bench.

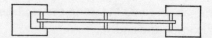

Inverted bench on jumping boxes (slotted)   FIG. 31

Jumping boxes can be used in conjunction with an inverted bench for the popular task of balance (Fig. 31 and Plate 28). These boxes are made in three sizes (12 in. high—small; 24 in. high—large; 36 in. high—extra large) and at one end a slot can be provided to receive the buttons of the inverted bench, thus making it safe and secure to use (Fig. 32).

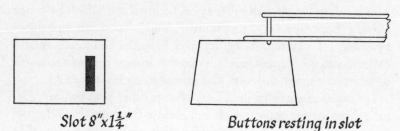

Slot 8"x1¼"   *Buttons resting in slot*

FIG. 32

Tasks based on balance—a few examples

   (a) Balance with an awareness of the part of the body on which the movement is done.
   (b) Balance with an awareness of body shape.
   (c) Moving balance as distinct from static balance.

148

(d) Sequences on appropriate apparatus including balance.
(e) Sequences based on balance.
(f) Partner balance, i.e. matching movements or supporting a partner's body weight in a position of balance on apparatus.
(g) Partner sequences including balance or based entirely on it.

The teacher must think of varied problems for the children to solve, and must present situations which will test and demand their skill and imagination. All these situations can be further modified by the factors of speed and direction, and also by the shape or position of the body.

Group work in a limited space

It is a fallacy to assume that it is impossible to organise successful group work in schools where only a small area of space is available. Both indoor and outdoor lessons can be made thoroughly active, purposeful and enjoyable in spite of cramped conditions if the apparatus is sited sensibly and if every bit of available space is used.

Overleaf is a diagram of the group arrangements in a school hall 35 feet long and 22 feet wide where some really excellent work was produced.

Group 1 2 rubber landing mats (4 ft × 3 ft) (partner practices).
      2 Wooden trestle, inclined bench and landing mat (4 ft × 3 ft).
      3 Wooden pole and tripod stands.
      4 Inverted bench and wooden trestle (balance work).
      5 Junior vaulting box, vaulting stool and 2 landing mats (4 ft × 3 ft).
      6 Climbing frame.
      7 Jumping boxes and 2 landing mats (4 ft × 3 ft).
      8 No apparatus (individual and partner work, balance).
      9 Wooden blocks and canes. 10 Parallel ropes.

Making the best use of existing facilities

Where space is very limited unusual ways of fixing equipment can often be found so that the best possible use is made of the

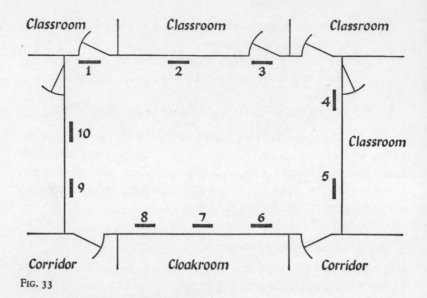

Classroom Classroom Classroom

1 2 3

4

10 Classroom

9 5

8 7 6

Corridor Cloakroom Corridor

Fig. 33

existing facilities. Plate 35 shows the very ingenious way in which three types of climbing apparatus have been successfully installed.

Summary and final comments

1 Though the first part of the lesson is important, group work provides the real application of all that has been learnt and should be thrilling, stimulating, challenging and enjoyable.
2 Careful preparation is essential—without this, progress will be limited and the satisfaction of both teacher and class seriously curtailed. Careful and imaginative siting of the equipment is an important feature of this planning.
3 Training in how to handle the apparatus is most important.
4 The teaching sequence to be followed when introducing and developing work on apparatus should be:

(a) exploration to gain confidence in the apparatus;
(b) demonstration and observation;
(c) repetition and consolidation;
(d) stimulation and coaching;
(e) imposing appropriate tasks or limitations.

5 The teacher should pass from group to group coaching, encouraging and stimulating as required, but when general points are being made, the whole class should listen.

6 In spite of the emphasis on free practice and exploration during group work, control of the class must be maintained at all times and the children must be trained to work quietly. The problems of discipline are minimised when children are busily occupied and apparatus work is varied and challenging.

7 The introduction, at the appropriate stage, of opportunities for partner and group co-operation produces stimulating and exciting work and is extremely popular with the children. The work is made still more interesting by the use of sequence work, individually, with a partner or in small groups.

8 Frequent changes in the apparatus arrangement in each group or in the planning as a whole are unnecessary. Ample opportunities for exploration and repetition are essential.

9 The successful teacher will stimulate the class towards improved quality and increased variety. Suggestion and help, individually and collectively, together with recognition of each child's progress will help to achieve both these aims.

10 Suitable footwear is essential for safety in group work unless facilities are suitable for work in bare feet. Stocking-feet, torn or worn plimsolls, and excessive clothing are dangerous.

11 Perhaps the most revolutionary change in the use of large apparatus in both Primary and Secondary work has been the acceptance of the principle which permits children to choose their own activities and to explore freely. This is thought by many to be a dangerous practice but experience has proved them wrong. As is stated in the Ministry of Education publication *Planning the Programme*:

'Responsibility for the safety of the children in their charge naturally weighs heavily on most teachers. Anxiety is sometimes acute because children are encouraged to play freely on apparatus of various kinds; yet this is only an extension to older age groups of the kind of thing that has been practised in nursery schools (with their climbing frames, ladders, chutes, etc.) for many years.'

CHAPTER 9

The Use of Small Apparatus

General considerations

There is a current idea that the use of small equipment in the P.E. lesson is outdated. We believe the contrary, and in previous chapters have tried to show its importance. Young children derive both pleasure and satisfaction from activities with small apparatus, and through its use teachers and children gain confidence in the new approach to gymnastics and learn relevant vocabulary and terms more quickly. Many practices with small equipment prompt ideas which can be implemented when large apparatus is later introduced. We hope, therefore, that a chapter devoted to suggestions for using different types of small apparatus may prove helpful.

All the items of small apparatus mentioned in Chapter 2 have been found to be valuable, notably:

(*a*) at the beginning of the lesson (introductory practices);

(*b*) in group work, especially where large apparatus is limited;

(*c*) as aids to the teacher when dealing with other phases of the lesson, e.g. running, jumping, landing, twisting, stretching, etc. These aspects have been referred to in more detail in other chapters.

Here we shall refer more particularly to those phases of the lesson in which the teacher is giving particular attention to increasing the ability and skill of the individual child when using the apparatus, or to providing opportunities for the children to widen their experience with the apparatus and to increase their own individual repertoire. The teacher's main function is to set the scene or create the situation in which the child can practise. He then makes use of the situations so created to accomplish the improvement or progress required. Though no particular point in the lesson plan is specifically set apart for this type of work, it is probably better done either just before the group work (class activity) or as part of the introductory phase. There is no hard and fast rule. The teacher will decide the most appropriate time for these practices, bearing in mind that time should not be wasted in changing too frequently from one piece of apparatus to the next. He should also ensure that sufficient time is allowed in order to make practice with a particular piece of apparatus worth while.

Teaching method

The methods of presentation possible are:

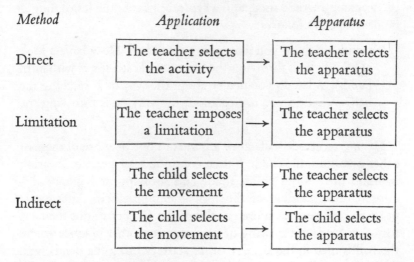

Method	Application	Apparatus
Direct	The teacher selects the activity →	The teacher selects the apparatus
Limitation	The teacher imposes a limitation →	The teacher selects the apparatus
Indirect	The child selects the movement →	The teacher selects the apparatus
	The child selects the movement →	The child selects the apparatus

It will be seen from the diagram that small apparatus will be used for one of three main purposes:

(a) to increase skill in particular specified activities;
(b) to give opportunity for exploration and for developing movements of a particular type;
(c) for a completely free choice of activity, when the main aims are to test whether the training has produced a wide repertoire, or to discover the kinds of activities which are appropriate to the age, inclination and ability of the class.

More often than not it will be found in practice that the coaching of a particular skill can lead into, or from, a phase of experimentation, e.g. free choice of activity where the ball is used on the ground could be followed by the specific practice of picking up a rolling ball, or vice versa, when picking up a rolling ball could be followed by other activities where the ball is used on the ground.

As in all other phases of the lesson the fullest use must be made of coaching by effective demonstration and intelligent observation, remembering the value of allowing the children to analyse, to appreciate differences, and to make comparisons for themselves, rather than having all the answers provided for them by the teacher. This exercise in discovery is a most important feature of the teaching method used, and a typical phase in the lesson might be developed as follows:

> 'Practise anything you like with a small ball. Now have a look at John (who is throwing the ball up and catching it with both hands). What do you notice about the way he is catching the ball? What do you notice about the way he is throwing the ball?'

Having received satisfactory answers to one or more of these or other questions, the children then continue their practice, bearing in mind the various points made and showing, it is hoped, increased understanding of the movement practised. After more practice, and perhaps more coaching, the teacher might then ask for other kinds of throwing or catching, any other practice where the ball is used in the air, any other activity using the hands with the ball, etc., all of which will be affected by the coaching already done. And so the lesson proceeds from one phase to another, the presentation and technique varying according to the discretion of the teacher and the needs of the class.

Small balls

A small ball is extremely valuable because skill in ball handling is essential to many games, a wide variety of activities is possible, and the small ball lends itself readily to informal teaching and experimentation. Small balls are very useful when teachers are using the Indirect Method of teaching for the first time, because children are normally so familiar with them.

There are several types of small balls available. If we were asked to make a general recommendation with regard to their relative merits we would say that the tennis ball is the best for all general purposes—it bounces well and truly, retains its shape and bounce, wears well and is pleasing to handle. The inflated rubber ball often loses its bounce quite quickly and the sponge rubber ball, though bouncing well, does not always have a very long life because children find it comparatively easy to pick bits out of it with their fingers. It is appreciated that tennis balls are generally more expensive than the other kinds, but second-hand balls can often be bought very cheaply from tennis clubs and 'C' quality new balls are quite suitable, are relatively inexpensive and are certainly cheaper in the long run. It is very easy to mark tennis balls in team colours or to dip them completely in dye. This is a great help in organisation and when checking the apparatus at the end of a lesson.

Gamester balls are also very popular and useful. They are made of plastic, have holes in them and can be thrown or hit quite hard, so they are particularly useful for partner practices inside and hitting practices outside.

Though a specific practice by the whole class will sometimes be beneficial, it is generally recommended that the children should be allowed to work out their own ideas as a result of a suggestion or stimulus by the teacher. The following are some suitable examples:

With a small ball

1 Practise (a) any kind of activity;
        (b) throwing and catching;
        (c) bouncing;
        (d) using your hands;
        (e) using one hand;
        (f) using both hands;
        (g) using your feet;
        (h) using different parts of your body.

2 Practise any kind of activity
  (a) in the air;
  (b) on the floor;
  (c) on the move;
  (d) on the floor using hands;
  (e) on the floor using feet;
  (f) using your hands as a bat;
  (g) with a partner;
  (h) using a wall.

3 Practise (a) throwing and catching on the move;
  (b) bouncing and catching on the move;
  (c) bouncing on the move;
  (d) bouncing combined with other activities;
  (e) catching combined with other activities.

With reference to the first example ('Practise any kind of activity with a small ball'), it should be noted that sometimes this can have a limited value because of the tendency for individual children to practise the same activity all the time. By careful guidance the teacher can avoid this and stimulate greater variety by asking the children to:

1 Practise something different;
2 Vary, in some way, whatever they are doing;
3 Add one movement to another;
or 4 Make a pattern or sequence.

It is interesting to note, in due course, not only the great variety which each child will exhibit, but the high standard of performance which is achieved, and it is recommended that the teacher should return to this indirect approach from time to time.

Types of small ball practices

The many types of small ball practices can be summarised under the following headings, but it is felt sufficiently important to repeat once more the recommendation that with all of these practices the children must be allowed freedom to interpret or answer the task or problem set in their own individual and varied ways. The teacher must be prepared to accept that there could be as many different ways of bouncing a ball as there are children in the class and even when further limitations are imposed (e.g. bouncing the ball on the move at different speeds), each child can be expected to find a different but equally satisfactory answer to the problem.

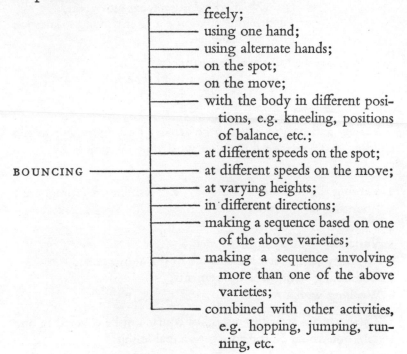

BOUNCING
- freely;
- using one hand;
- using alternate hands;
- on the spot;
- on the move;
- with the body in different positions, e.g. kneeling, positions of balance, etc.;
- at different speeds on the spot;
- at different speeds on the move;
- at varying heights;
- in different directions;
- making a sequence based on one of the above varieties;
- making a sequence involving more than one of the above varieties;
- combined with other activities, e.g. hopping, jumping, running, etc.

The following are a few examples of the many kinds of activities which will emerge when children are given opportunity to work out ideas on the lines of these suggestions:

1 Bouncing and catching.
2 Bouncing and catching on the move.
3 Pat-bouncing (tall body, loose hand, controlled movements).
4 Pat-bouncing (*a*) using alternate hands,
　　　　　　 (*b*) making patterns—the ball moves round the child,
　　　　　　 (*c*) making patterns—the child moves round the ball,
　　　　　　 (*d*) using one hand on the move,
　　　　　　 (*e*) using both hands on the move,

(f) in a position of balance,
(g) in different positions,
(h) in different positions of balance,
(i) in different positions on the move,
(j) with any kind of jumping movement,
(k) changing position, e.g. from standing to kneeling to sitting, etc.

5 Bouncing the ball across to a partner:
(a) 1 ball between 2,
(b) 1 ball each.

Variety and progression can be achieved by suggesting to the children that they could develop what they are doing, by:

1 Using both hands;
2 Varying the position of the body, e.g. standing, kneeling, etc.;
3 Bouncing on the move;
4 Variation of speed;
5 Variation of direction;
6 Making patterns involving some of the above ideas;
7 Combining with other movements;
8 Working with a partner.

These various activities would of course not be covered in one lesson, but would be spread over several lessons.

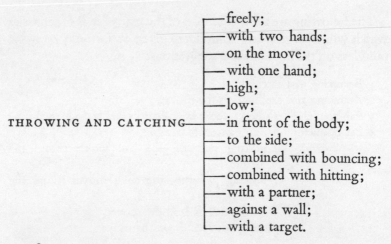

THROWING AND CATCHING——
— freely;
— with two hands;
— on the move;
— with one hand;
— high;
— low;
— in front of the body;
— to the side;
— combined with bouncing;
— combined with hitting;
— with a partner;
— against a wall;
— with a target.

1 Throwing and catching using both hands (stationary). This is an essential preliminary stage.

Technique (a) Throw the ball up with one hand (much bad catching is due to poor throwing—the hand should follow the ball into the air).

(b) Watch the ball all the time.

(c) Get 'underneath' the ball quickly so that if possible you are not moving at the moment of catching.

(d) Make a cup with the hands.

(e) Go to meet the ball with the hands.

(f) Follow through with the hands towards the body (the 'squash' part of catching).

2 Practise any kind of throwing and catching.

3 Throwing and catching using one hand.

4 Throwing and catching on the move.

5 Throw with one hand—catch with the other.

6 Throwing and catching with a partner: (a) 1 ball between 2;
(b) 1 ball each;
(c) on the move.

7 Throwing and catching practice against a wall.

8 Throwing practice against a wall—let the ball bounce and then catch it.

9 Throwing in varying directions and running to catch.

10 Throwing for distance (where space permits or with stocking or gamester balls).

Variety and progression can be achieved by using one hand instead of two; practising on the move; combining with other activities; working with a partner; using a wall; or using other apparatus, e.g. a hoop, a bat, blocks, or skittles.

During free practice of throwing and catching the children should be encouraged to catch efficiently in a variety of ways and their practices should be directed to this end. They should be encouraged to catch high, low, to the right or left, at chest height, knee height, waist height, at the top of the bounce, near the floor, and so on. This can be applied to almost all the throwing and catching practices, either with one hand or both.

From experience teachers will find that a much greater variety of suitable activities will be produced by the children than at first would appear possible, even when a limited choice of activity is allowed, e.g. 'Use the ball with your hands, on the move.' Such a task will produce such activities as: throwing and catching; bouncing and catching; pat-bouncing along the floor; hand dribbling the ball on the floor; fielding a rolling ball; combinations of these.

All types of ball practices against a wall are recommended and especially during outdoor lessons, when throwing and catching practices against a suitable wall will give additional opportunities for hard throwing and training in good footwork.

Individual mats

The value of individual rubber mats has now been generally accepted and cannot be over-emphasised; suggestions for using them have been made in several chapters. Many of the activities suggested for foot and ankle training, for jumping and landing practices, for body movements and for activities on the hands, depend to a large extent upon the provision of mats of this type. It is sufficient here to refer in general terms only to ideas or suggestions for the miscellaneous uses of this apparatus. Each of these suggestions will lead to a number of activities and a considerable variety of movements. From this variety the teacher can select particular activities for class coaching and practice, or a type of movement which allows for further exploration and individual choice. In addition, the teacher could select a particular feature which the class would then be asked to emphasise or concentrate upon (e.g. lightness), while at the same time the children could remain free to choose within the range of their own ability.

For example, the teacher might ask the class to practise any activity or movement over the mat. Some will jump over, some will go over using their hands, some will roll over, and so on. Each one of these movements can be performed in many different ways so that the ultimate variety of movements produced will be considerable. A child who is moving over the mat taking his weight on his hands might be selected for demonstration purposes and the teacher could then ask the class to practise that particular activity,

45 'Jumping for joy'

46 Children enjoy inversion

47 Each 'task' can be solved in different ways

48 'Use your partner as a platform for balance'

if it is suitable for class practice, or to practise any activity over the mat using the hands. In either case the activities should be coached. Perhaps one of the points for coaching might be the lightness with which the movement is performed and after coaching this the teacher might then say, 'Practise any movement over the mat, concentrating on lightness.'

Suitable examples of tasks or limitations

1 Practise any kind of movement over (on, round, along) your mat.
2 Practise a running activity round your mat.
3 Practise a jumping activity on (round, over) your mat.
4 Practise jumps over your mat (deep landings with rebound).
5 Practise any activity (*a*) on your hands;
    (*b*) on your shoulders;
    (*c*) on your side;
    (*d*) on your front;
    (*e*) on your back;
    (*j*) on one hand;
    (*g*) over your mat, taking your weight on your hands.
6 Practise any (*a*) rolling activity;
    (*b*) rocking movement;
    (*c*) stretching and curling movement;
    (*d*) twisting and turning;
    (*e*) activity with your feet in the air;
    (*f*) bridge-like movement over (or round) your mat.
7 Practise any activity (*a*) round the mat using hands and feet on the floor;
    (*b*) where you go over the mat one way and return in another.
8 Practise any kind of stretching and curling movement on the mat.
9 Practise any kind of twisting and turning movement round the mat.
10 Practise any partner activity (with mats side by side).
11 Combine different movements on (or moving round) your mat.
12 Make a pattern or sequence of movements from any of the above (individually or with a partner).

Skipping ropes

Ropes may be used in the following ways:

1 For a completely free choice of activity;
2 For skipping activities;
3 For jumping practices;
4 For jumping and landing;
5 On the ground—long, circular, folded, etc.;
6 In knotted form—in one hand, two hands, on the ground, between the feet, etc.

Examples of suitable tasks

With a rope, practise: any movement or activity;
skipping;
jumping (rope on the ground);
jumping (rope held in the hands);
jumping and landing;
any activity (rope on the ground);
any activity (knotted rope);
any activity (knotted rope on the ground);
any activity (knotted rope held in the hands or feet).

Any one of these ideas can be further developed and teachers should employ the technique of watching the children and using ideas produced by them in order to obtain further development.

It will be sufficient to enlarge on one or two of these ideas to illustrate the variety of movements which children will produce in any or all of the various examples given. Suppose the teacher has said, 'Place your rope on the ground and show me anything you can do along, over, or round it.' First of all there will be the many ways in which the rope will have been placed on the ground (some will have stretched it out in a straight line, others will have made different shapes, e.g. letters of the alphabet, numbers, circles, etc.).

In addition, there will be a considerable variety of activities and movements which the children will produce. For example, some will run round, over and along their rope in different directions and at different speeds—some will jump, hop or skip in various ways, whilst others might move with their body weight on hands, or on hands and feet, etc. One thing should be remembered, that the variety of work produced, and the standard of performance reached in the various activities, will both be increased if opportunity is given for repetition of the same type of demands in the same or similar situation in later lessons. Children enjoy repetition, and building from one lesson to another should always be a feature of their work.

In a similar way, the teacher could decide to develop the 'skipping' type of movements with the rope and to do this the following tasks might be set:

Skipping practices

With a rope, practise: any kind of skipping;
skipping on both feet;
skipping on alternate feet;
running skipping;
hopping skipping;
slow skipping;
skipping showing variations in speed;
skipping emphasising lightness;
skipping emphasising 'stretch';
skipping making a pattern by combining different skipping movements;
skipping making a pattern with the feet or legs;
skipping in different directions;
skipping showing a change in direction;
skipping on the move;
skipping with a partner (for older children).

In Chapter 4 we dealt with the question of developing an idea and suggested stages by which this development could be carried out. This can be applied to a phase of skipping practices as to all other kinds of activities, as follows:

163

Stage 1 Practise any kind of skipping.

Stage 2 Find other ways of skipping.

(In addition to the children's own ideas, this stage will include the use of demonstration, observation and teacher stimulation.)

Stage 3 Combine some of these ways of skipping to make a pattern.

Stage 4 Practise your sequence and if necessary rearrange it to make the sequence more effective.

Stage 5 Add other skipping movements to make your sequence longer.

Teachers must remember that at *all* stages there will be need for demonstration, observation and stimulation related to both quality and variety.

As a final reminder of the opportunities presented at all stages for developing ideas, the following diagram will show the types of movements which can result from pursuing one line only:

'With the rope on the ground, show me what you can do *over* it.'

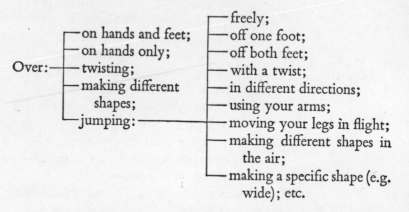

No matter what the movement is, what type of apparatus is used, or what task is set, there is apparently no end to the developments and variations possible.

Wooden blocks

These are blocks of light, soft wood, 12 inches by 3 inches by 3 inches, with a groove in one or both ends.

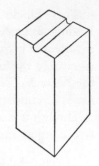

FIG. 34

They are used either singly, in pairs, threes, or fours, and sometimes in combination with canes, hoops or mats. They are valuable during the first part of the lesson either for individual practices or for class activities, and in group work during the second part of the lesson. Ideally there should be a sufficient number of these wooden blocks to allow one to be available for each child in the class—otherwise, if only a few are available, their usefulness is confined almost entirely to work by a small group of children during group work.

In Chapter 2 we explained the need for dispersal of small apparatus and for careful arrangements for storage—Figs. 1 and 2 and Plates 1 and 4 illustrate a typical arrangement of wooden blocks and other apparatus in 'team corners'.

If the blocks have to be moved frequently it is advisable to have boxes or containers of some kind in which to carry them.

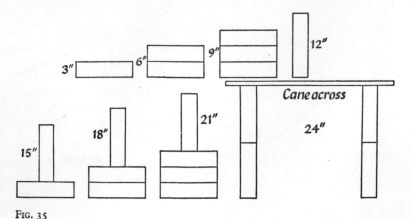

FIG. 35

These blocks have a particular value for running, jumping and landing practices in the first part of the lesson and for jumping practices in group work. Occasionally children should be allowed to change the arrangement of the blocks and alter the height of the obstacle. This is a distinct advantage when catering for the needs of children with varying ability.

Though it is advisable to leave the children to do the building, two dangers must be avoided:

(a) The children will tend to build too high an obstacle with the result that the blocks are continually knocked over.
(b) If the children are allowed to have too many blocks at once they will tend to build rather than jump.

It ought to be mentioned that the blocks can be used with equal satisfaction and success when built into patterns on the floor as well as in the air, so creating a different kind of situation. They can also be used to provide a series of obstacles on the hurdling pattern,

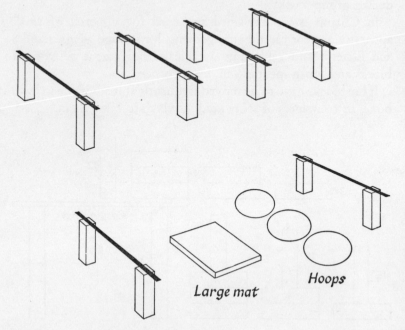

Large mat

Hoops

Fig. 36
166

i.e. canes across blocks in a series of regular intervals, or for a series of obstacles in combination with other kinds of small apparatus, as shown opposite (Fig. 36). Further variety can be obtained by altering the heights of the blocks (see Fig. 35).

It is perhaps wise to introduce children to these blocks by a rather more direct approach, giving the children more freedom of choice later when they have acquired some good ideas about the ways in which they can be used. It is not recommended that the teacher should say to the children when blocks are being used for the *first* time, 'Get a small block each and show me what you can do with it.' One of the first things the children must be taught is how to place the block *quietly* on the floor, and then it is wise for the teacher to suggest what comes next, for example:

(*a*) Show me how many ways you can jump over or round your block.

or (*b*) Show me some running round your block.

This might be followed by the request, 'Show me other ways of moving round your block.'

Since these blocks also fulfil, among other things, the purposes of an ordinary skittle, they constitute a very inexpensive and valuable piece of small apparatus.

Some suggestions for using wooden blocks

If the same teaching technique as has been suggested for other apparatus is employed, the following ideas will provide suitable starting-points for further expansion and development:

1 Practise any kind of running round your block.
2 Practise running freely between the blocks.
3 Practise any kind of jumping over or round your block.
4 Make a pattern of jumps over and round your block.
5 Practise jumps with leg movements in the air.
6 Practise jumps in different directions over the block.
7 Practise jumping making shapes in the air over the block.
8 Find ways of twisting round or over your block.
9 Practise making bridge-like shapes over or round your block.
10 Move round your block on your hands and feet.

11 Move round your block with all your weight on your hands.
12 Make a pattern or sequence of movements over or round your block.
13 With a cane across two blocks,
   (a) find ways of going over (under, over and under) the cane;
   (b) use your blocks and cane for jumping practices. (This activity would be suitable for group work, two or three blocks being placed on top of each other.)

Playbats and gamester balls

These are mostly used in games lessons during the introductory phase and in group work, and provide very interesting and valuable practices. Teachers should not overlook the value of playing with a bat and ball, and the skill associated with it, even in indoor work.

Some suggestions (mostly for outdoor lessons)
1 Individual practice—keeping the ball in the air,
   (a) where you are;
   (b) on the move;
   (c) moving in different directions;
   (d) at different heights.
2 Playbat and a ball between two children—one hits and the partner catches.
3 Playbat and a ball between two children—one serves and the partner hits.
4 Playbat each—one ball between two children (keeping the ball in the air).
5 Playbat each—one ball between two children in a small court, with two skittles or blocks and a cane to act as a net.

Hoops

Many activities with hoops are possible indoors, but activities of the running and bowling type are more suitable in the playground. Children devise many interesting activities as a result of suggestions such as the following:

Practise (*a*) any kind of activity with a hoop;
       (*b*) any kind of activity with the hoop on the floor;
       (*c*) any jumping activity with the hoop;
       (*d*) any jumping activity with the hoop on the floor;
       (*e*) any jumping activity round the hoop;
       (*f*) any jumping activity in and out of the hoop;
       (*g*) any jumping activity over the hoop;
       (*h*) any activity on your hands using the hoop on the
            floor;
       (*i*) any circling activity with the hoop (round the arm,
            leg or body);
       (*j*) any activity with a partner.

Summary

The following is a summary of the many ways in which the small apparatus can be used in the various phases of the lesson:

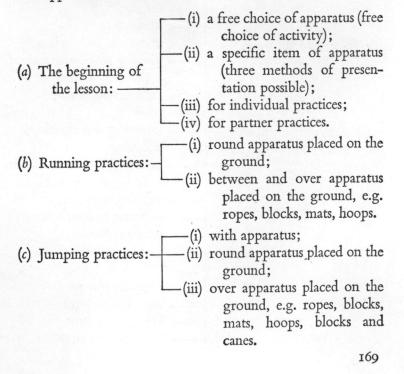

(*a*) The beginning of the lesson:
- (i) a free choice of apparatus (free choice of activity);
- (ii) a specific item of apparatus (three methods of presentation possible);
- (iii) for individual practices;
- (iv) for partner practices.

(*b*) Running practices:
- (i) round apparatus placed on the ground;
- (ii) between and over apparatus placed on the ground, e.g. ropes, blocks, mats, hoops.

(*c*) Jumping practices:
- (i) with apparatus;
- (ii) round apparatus placed on the ground;
- (iii) over apparatus placed on the ground, e.g. ropes, blocks, mats, hoops, blocks and canes.

169

(d) Body movements:
    (i) on mats:
- rocking;
- rolling;
- stretching
- curling;
- twisting;
- arching;
- on the front,
  the side,
  the back,
  the shoulders,
  different body parts;
- taking the body weight;
- transferring the body weight;
- wide shapes;
- long shapes;
- bridge-like shapes.

    (ii) round apparatus:
- twisting;
- rolling;
- stretching;
- stretching and curling;
- moving from one part of the body to another;
- different body shapes.

(e) Arm movements:
- skipping;
- throwing and catching;
- bouncing;
- taking the weight of the body on the hands.

(f) Weight on the hands:
- running movements;
- jumping movements;
- with the feet high;
- making specific shapes with the legs;
- over apparatus;
- round apparatus;
- along apparatus;
- bridge-like shapes.

(g) Class activity or phases of training, such as ball practices; skipping; partner practices.
(h) Group work: (i) as group activities—individual or partner;
(ii) to supplement large apparatus.

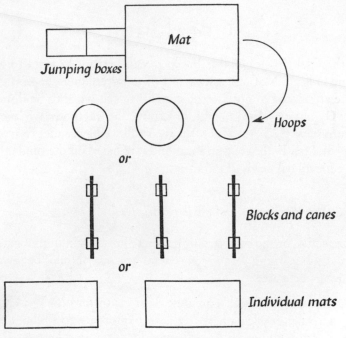

Fig. 37

171

CHAPTER 10

Conclusion

In the final chapter of this book, it will perhaps be wise to give some indication of our assessment of the preceding chapters. We have attempted to outline the content of the work to be done in the Gymnastics lesson, and described the methods we would recommend teachers to use. But above all we have endeavoured to explain how both work and methods are based on the fundamental educational needs of children.

The learning process and basic principles

Irrespective of the subject taught, there are certain ingredients of successful learning of which every teacher should be aware. Among these are:

(a) *Exploration.* 'Man's greatest desire is to find out'—a child's first inclination with a new toy is to explore its possibilities, and then to find out how it works; these instincts must be catered for by the provision of opportunities for exploration in physical activity during the Physical Education lesson.

(b) *Thought.* Children should be trained to think about what they are doing, and to think independently. This is appropriate in the Physical Education lesson, also, when the teacher should encourage in the child the ability to think, and to use and develop his initiative, imagination and inventiveness, rather than always telling the child exactly what to do.

(c) *Repetition and consolidation.* Both are necessary in any learning process. Children enjoy repetition and need to repeat movements over and over again in order to master them.

(d) *Help and guidance.* All children require some help and one of the teacher's main functions is to give help and guidance as and when required. Children appreciate the help they receive from an understanding teacher.

(e) *Stimulation and encouragement*. Both are essential if the interest and enthusiasm of the children are to be maintained.

(f) *Effort*. The children must always be encouraged to make the greatest effort of which they are capable.

(g) *Security*. Children must be made to feel secure in order that they may develop a sense of adequacy to cope with the situations in which they find themselves, and to solve satisfactorily the many problems set. This sense of adequacy can only be achieved satisfactorily if the methods employed cater for the individual child and permit opportunities for some degree of choice.

(h) *Achievement*. Irrespective of the child's physique or physical ability, the teacher's main aim should be to ensure that every child in the class does in fact experience, as often as possible, a sense of achievement. Without this there can be little interest, no enthusiasm and limited progress. In any teaching situation the ultimate test of the teacher's success is the reaction of the children to him and to his subject.

(i) *Progress*. It is essential that both teacher and children should feel that progress is being made. The teacher must appreciate and understand that progress is individual to each child.

(j) *Understanding*. This point has been purposely left to the last because of its importance. Teacher and children must understand not only *what* they are doing, but also *how* and *why* they are doing it. The traditional teaching method, whereby the children were always told exactly what to do, did not always accomplish this.

The teacher

To ensure that the best use is made of the material at his or her disposal the teacher must possess and develop certain qualities, endeavouring:

(a) to be as knowledgeable as possible;
(b) to apply the principles involved intelligently;
(c) to be enthusiastic;
(d) to be willing to learn;
(e) to be willing to experiment;

173

(f) to be sympathetic with the difficulties which some children experience;

(g) to be aware of the differences between children and to appreciate that they vary as much in physical ability as they do in mental ability;

(h) to vary the method of presentation used to cater for these differences;

(i) to establish good class–teacher relationship, i.e. a happy atmosphere of willing co-operation;

(j) to appreciate the need for discipline based on interest and individual self-control;

(k) to appreciate the need for personal effort and consistently good teaching;

(l) to make thorough preparation, and appreciate the need for sound and efficient organisation;

(m) to be ambitious and demand worthwhile standards, remembering that children will give what is demanded of them;

(n) to give each child an opportunity to experience a sense of achievement;

(o) to believe sincerely in the aims of the subject.

(p) to set a good example at all times to those whom he teaches.

Progression—methods of development

One of the problems which has concerned teachers in the development of modern work has been with regard to the much discussed term 'progression'. This is perhaps an unfortunate term to use in relation to the development of the work from day to day, but it is difficult to find a more suitable expression to describe the opportunities afforded to each individual to improve his physical ability in the widest sense.

In general terms, progression covers (a) improvement in the quality of performance; (b) increased variety and versatility in the individual; and (c) greater understanding of what is being done.

The quality of performance of any movement can be improved by increasing the range of the movement, and by perfecting the style or technique; in other words, by a more skilful execution of the activity being performed. Further development of skill and understanding can also be obtained by learning how to perform the same type of movement in a variety of ways—for example, different ways of running, or jumping, or taking or transferring weight, and so on. The many ways in which this variety manifests itself have been dealt with in various parts of this book, and in particular in Chapter 4. Each child must be encouraged to perform as wide a variety of movements as possible and to become skilful and confident in the use of all types of small and large apparatus.

Further progress is obtained by:

(a) increasing the degree of limitation,
> e.g. practice of jumping freely, later jumping with a turn of the body; skipping freely, later skipping at varying speeds, etc.;

(b) combining two or more different types of movements to form a pattern or sequence,
> e.g. stretching–balancing–rolling, etc.;

(c) endeavouring to link movements and activities in a smooth continuous sequence, demanding effective arrangement;

(d) co-operating with a partner in a variety of ways,
> e.g. as a helper, as a piece of apparatus or in 'matching' movements;

(e) co-operating as a member of a group.

Progression is very much an individual matter and the teacher must remember that the improvement of a class is only the reflection of the progress made by the individual children within it. The rate of progress will vary from child to child and from class to class so that the teacher must not expect to be able to decide in advance that a particular stage will be reached by a certain date. It will often be found that younger classes and children make more rapid progress in some directions than older ones.

Standards of work

Once the principle of progression has been accepted, then the principle that standards of work are important must also be accepted. There are, however, some differences these days in the ways in which standards of work are assessed. It will be apparent from all that has been written in this book, that it is no longer enough to produce a high standard of performance in a few selected activities. It is still important, when a child is attempting any particular activity, to demand as high a standard of performance as the child can produce, but the real merits of a class are now assessed with many other factors in mind. These factors have been dealt with frequently and include, among others, the principles behind the work, the aims involved, the atmosphere created, the preparations made, the varied methods of presentation adopted, the consistent effort of each child, the amount of activity, the standards of changing, the care and use of the apparatus, and the progress made by each individual child both in the quality and in the variety of his work. The important point to remember is that the teacher sets the standard to be reached by the demands he or she makes upon the class, and many classes which appear to be doing satisfactory work could in fact do very much better if only the teacher's standards were higher. In addition, it is true to say that when children have left school they will recall their Physical Education lessons with pleasure and satisfaction if the standards demanded of them have been appropriate and adequate.

Games training

Although this book has been chiefly concerned with the content and method of the Gymnastics lesson, we are no less anxious to ensure that children in Primary Schools should enjoy opportunities to participate in effective games lessons. It is our opinion that the principles and methods of presentation suggested for the teaching of Gymnastics apply equally to games lessons, where the aim should be to present a lesson full of purposeful activity related to the age, ability and experience of the child, and one which offers the maximum opportunity for play and practice.

In the games lesson there should be evidence of a lesson plan which provides for individual, partner and group work, and variety in the method of presentation which will facilitate free practice, some opportunity for choice and experimentation, together with coaching by the teacher on the lines suggested in

49 'Use the ball in the air'

50 'Change your position as you bounce the ball'

51 Small apparatus adds interest and purpose to the work

52 The children are stimulated to find new ways of using their apparatus

Chapter 3. Teaching techniques, involving the use of demonstration, observation and other teaching aids, can be used with equal success in the games lesson. If teachers conduct their games lessons in this way, and concentrate more on small-side games and practices than full-size team matches, the standard of games in Primary Schools will undoubtedly be considerably improved.

We suggest that teachers would be wise to follow the maxim 'Play a little—teach a little!' Games lessons should not lack the play element, should include the element of competition, should provide the maximum opportunity for practice and should leave room for the maximum amount of help and guidance to be given by the teacher. As much care should be given to the preparation and organisation of a games lesson and the apparatus to be used as is given to the preparation of a lesson in Gymnastics.

Safety precautions

Some teachers express concern about the safety precautions which they should observe when conducting Gymnastics lessons on the less formal lines associated with modern work. As in all lessons the teacher must ensure that the facilities and apparatus used are as safe as possible, and that the chances of injury or accident from furniture, slippery floors, etc., have been reduced to a minimum. The need for children to be suitably clothed and either adequately shod or barefoot (where conditions permit) is specially important in view of the much greater use now being made of large apparatus. Under no circumstances should children be allowed to participate if socks or stockings are their only form of footwear, because this is very dangerous.

Where it has been difficult to persuade children to change properly for Physical Education lessons, experience has shown that one of the quickest ways to improve the situation is to conduct a demonstration lesson specially for parents. They are invariably so enthusiastic about what they see, and so appreciative of the points made with regard to the necessity for adequate changing, that improvement invariably and immediately results.

The main cause for concern is in the use of the fixed, portable and improvised apparatus used in group work. Reference to some of the safety precautions necessary has already been made in Chapter 8 where teachers were advised to ensure that the apparatus was safe to use, and to site it in order to avoid collisions with walls, doors, furniture, other apparatus or other children.

But the main safety precaution lies in the method of presentation used. In the early stages children should be given freedom to explore and thus gain confidence; later they should be encouraged to build on the confidence and experience gained, but should still be allowed some degree of freedom to choose their own activities within whatever limits the teacher wishes to set. In such circumstances nothing should be done to disturb the confidence of the children. This is quite a different situation from that which obtains when the activity is directed by the teacher, and we have already indicated that we do not consider the direct approach to be suitable for work with large apparatus. Class control is essential at all times and if the work has been developed on the lines suggested and the children work in small groups, there should be no problems of discipline. The teacher should use common sense to see that the children are not unnecessarily exposed to danger; allow them freedom to choose, and see that they are not being foolish in their choice; avoid any element of competition so that the child is not urged to do something more difficult than he is capable of doing, and give every encouragement to the children to be sensible, confident and self-reliant.

Schemes of work and lesson preparation

Teachers frequently ask for advice in planning a scheme of work to cover a week, a month, a term, or even a year. The work described in this book represents a scheme of work for the whole of the Primary-School age group and it is impracticable to prepare a detailed scheme of activities which will be appropriate for a particular class at any particular time. A scheme should therefore give an indication only of the outline plan which the teacher intends to follow, so that preparation and organisation of apparatus can be carried out, leaving the actual work to evolve lesson by lesson. We have shown how this development can take place in each phase of the lesson, and we have dealt with progression earlier in this chapter, so that the following outline of a scheme for a period of a month or even half a term will perhaps be a sufficient guide for the preparation of similar schemes. (A school with average facilities and an average supply of equipment is envisaged in this hypothetical scheme.)

CLASS III   FEBRUARY–MARCH

Part I

INTRODUCTORY PRACTICES

1 (a) Free practice with a free choice of small apparatus.
   (b) Variety encouraged.
   (c) Combined movements—sequences.
2 (a) Skipping practice—combine two or more variations.
   (b) Sequences of skipping—both quick and slow movements.
   (c) Free practice with the rope on the ground.
   (d) As in (c) but different ways of moving over the rope.
3 (a) Sequences without apparatus.
   (b) As in (a) but sequences to include (i) a position of balance;
                                         (ii) an inverted movement.

RUNNING

Variation of speed and change of direction.

JUMPING AND LANDING

1 (a) Freely—using a hoop on the ground.
   (b) Variety stimulated.
   (c) Related to variation in take-off.
   (d) With inclusion of a twist or turn in flight.
2 (a) About the hall without apparatus—feet as high as possible off the ground.
   (b) With additional movements on landing.
         (Footwork practices where applicable.)

BODY MOVEMENTS

1 (a) Combine different ways of bridging and arching.
   (b) As in (a) but include (i) a bridge-like balance;
                             (ii) a moving bridge-like shape.
2 On shoulders—a combination of quick and slow movements.

WEIGHT-BEARING ON THE HANDS

(a) Moving about the hall taking body weight on the hands.
(b) Balance on hands.   (c) Combine (a) and (b).

BALANCE

(a) A combination of stretched and curled balance positions.
(b) Partner balance (different ways).

CLASS ACTIVITY

(a) Ways of jumping over partners (human apparatus).
(b) Free partner co-operation.

Part II

GROUP WORK

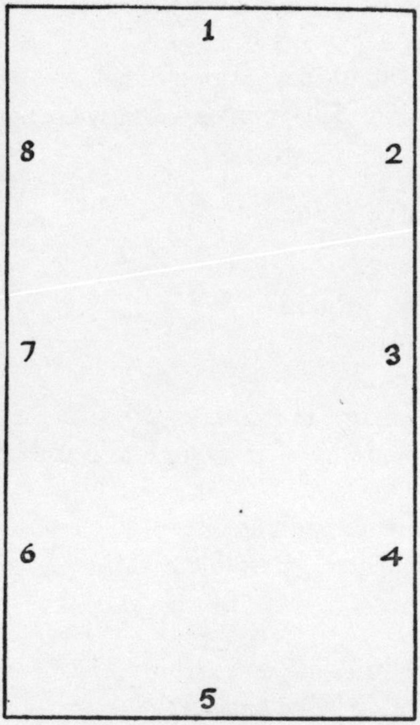

FIG. 38

APPARATUS AND TASK

1 Inverted bench on jumping boxes—free practice.
2 Skipping ropes—partner or group skipping.
3 Pole and stands—balance and rolling.
4 Inclined bench on trestle, two 4 ft by 3 ft mats, 3 hoops—flight and rolling.
5 Two 4 ft by 3 ft mats—partner balance.
6 Blocks and canes (1 set each)—ways of moving over.
7 Climbing frame—ways of hanging, stretching and arching.
8 Jumping boxes (2 small, 2 large), two 4 ft by 3 ft mats, skittles on canes—free practice but with variation of direction and shape.

For the normal week to week preparation a pro forma similar to Fig. 39 is recommended. Cyclostyled copies might be made available by the Head Teacher for completion and inclusion in the teacher's record book.

As discussed in Chapter 4 and as recommended in the lesson plan (Fig. 9) details of the tasks imposed need only be given for the phases of work actually undertaken. The phases not being dealt with will, therefore, be left blank.

It will be appreciated that consecutive lessons will bear a marked resemblance to each other, the main difference being the normal progress made between one lesson and the next. Such progress involves, among other things, the development of new ideas and improvement in the quality and standard of performance.

Class: **Week beginning:**

Part I		Part II	
Phase	**Detail**	**Group**	**Activities**
Intro		Group	Apparatus and task
R-J-L		1	
		2	
B. Mvt.		3	
		4	
Bal.		5	
		6	
Wt. on Hds.		7	
C. Act.		8 etc.	

Fig. 39

Three typical lessons

Finally, we would like to give details of three typical lessons, each of which was developed over several weeks and eventually demonstrated at a course for teachers.

Readers will appreciate:

(*a*) That these are suggestions only and are not intended to be followed identically, because each teacher will plan and develop the work individually, relative to the facilities available and to the class being taught.

(*b*) That these lessons contain more material than would be included in a normal lesson because of the desire to show as many ideas and as much work as possible to the teachers attending the course.

(*c*) That we have, in some places, included for their guidance, in parenthesis, an indication of the particular aim or teaching technique involved at that particular time in the lesson.

Lesson demonstrated by a class aged 8–9 years

Part I

THE INTRODUCTORY PHASE

In this lesson the apparatus chosen is a small ball, and progress has been as follows:

1 Practise quite *freely* with your ball. (The Indirect Method of presentation.)

   When using this method the teacher should stimulate both quality and variety of movement. It must be realised that if the children are left entirely to themselves, without the guidance, help and stimulation of the teacher, the work becomes very limited.

2 *Combine* several movements with the ball and ultimately arrange into a sequence.

3 Include in your sequence one high and one low movement. (A combination of the Indirect and Limitation Methods of presentation.)

4 Practise throwing with one hand and catching with both hands. (Here the teacher imposes on the class the activity to be practised and is therefore using the Direct Method of presentation.)

182

Running

1 Running practice 'on the spot'—concentrating on lightness and good footwork. (Basic footwork practices also help.)
2 Running about the hall—concentrating on:
   (*a*) Good use of space;
   (*b*) Style;
   (*c*) Variation of speed.

Jumping and Landing

1 Practise jumping and landing—over small apparatus, e.g. a
                                 wooden block
                              —moving about the hall

   (*a*) concentrating on lightness in take-off and landing (Quality);
   (*b*) concentrating on height (Quality);
   (*c*) showing different body shapes or positions (Variety).

2 Show *long* body shapes in flight. (Increasing the degree of limitation.)
3 How many different ways can you do this? (Variety.)

Normally in one lesson, one way of dealing with jumping and landing in Part I is sufficient. In this lesson, however, it is presented with and without apparatus, and it is also possible to present jumping practices in twos with partners acting as the apparatus. This method is extremely popular with older children and is more economical in terms of space because only half of the class is jumping at any given time. Human apparatus offers many advantages, e.g. the height and position of the body can be changed quickly, such variations often prompting different kinds of jumps. Moreover, this practice can serve as a useful basis for other and more advanced aspects of partner work.

BODY MOVEMENT

Stretching

1 Practise different ways of stretching.
2 Move from one way to another.
3 Arrange into a sequence.

If space permits it will be seen that the jumping and landing practised earlier in the lesson can be linked with the sequence developed in this phase, e.g. 'Devise a sequence based on stretching and begin with or include a jumping movement where the body shape is long.'

BALANCE

Balance presents a most interesting challenge to children. It involves taking, supporting or moving body weight on one or more small parts of the body. It demands control and the task can be undertaken on an individual or partner basis, the latter preferably for older children.

The teaching sequence—one way, other ways, etc.—can be used here with considerable success, but the children should be given ample opportunity for experimentation, i.e. 'Find *different* ways of balancing.'

It will be found that the children's skill and inventiveness within this aspect of activity, as elsewhere in Part I of the lesson, will be applied to the more interesting and challenging situations which can be created through the use of large apparatus in group work.

Part II

GROUP WORK

The planning and content of group work is influenced by the *space* and range of *apparatus* available, and the *number* of children in the class, etc. In this lesson the following arrangement of apparatus was used (Fig. 40).

Lesson demonstrated by a class aged 9–10 years

Part I

THE INTRODUCTORY PHASE (A)

Apparatus—Ropes

'Practise a sequence composed of different kinds of skipping movements.' Development has been as follows:

1 Practise any *one* kind of skipping movement—the teacher

184

coaches for qualities of lightness, good footwork, smooth
continuous movement of the rope, etc.

2 Practise *other* kinds of skipping—here the teacher stimulates
variety:

Primary school hall (37ft×31ft)

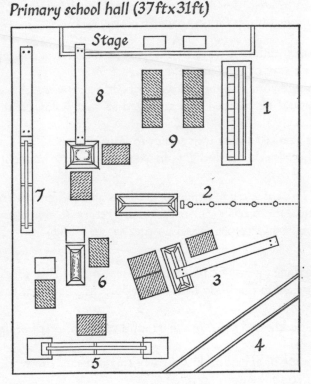

Fig. 40

group	apparatus
1	Climbing frame.
2	Ropes, trestle.
3	Trestle, inclined bench, three mats.
4	Parallel ropes.
5	Two large jumping boxes, inverted bench, mat.
6	Vaulting box, two small jumping boxes, two mats.
7	Two benches (one inverted).
8	Vaulting stool, two mats, bench (from stage to stool).
9	Two small jumping boxes (on stage), four mats.

(a) by allowing opportunity for *experimentation*;
(b) through the medium of *demonstration* (watching each other);
(c) through the *question and answer* technique;
(d) through *demonstration, observation, and comment* (Why or how is this different from that?);
(e) by *relating* the skipping to *an additional factor*, e.g. speed, direction, position, partner co-operation.

3 *Combine* different ways of skipping; OR Can you change from one way of skipping to another?
4 Arrange your skipping movements into a *sequence*. (A sequence should be planned and arranged so that it can be repeated exactly.)
5 Can you *add* a new movement to your sequence? OR Can you *rearrange* the movements in your sequence to make it more effective?

N.B. To encourage experimentation and extension of the sequence, the teacher can occasionally return to Stage 2 of this teaching sequence, i.e. 'Devise other ways.'

ALTERNATIVE INTRODUCTORY PHASE (B) (This idea could also be used in the Body Movement phase of the lesson.)

1 Over a knotted rope on the ground make different bridge-like shapes.
(The use of apparatus in the early stages makes the work more interesting and objective.)
2 Can you move more effectively from one to another?
3 Plan a sequence based on this idea.

The same task can also be imposed without apparatus, allowing the children greater freedom of movement and more space. To increase the demand upon the children and to stimulate even greater variety, the children are challenged, progressively, to include in their bridging and arching sequences:

(a) one that is wide;
(b) one that is long;

(c) one that is twisted;
(d) one that is upside down or inverted;
(e) one that moves.

This method of development is known as 'increasing the degree of limitation' or 'relating a subsidiary factor to the main task'.

THE RUNNING, JUMPING AND LANDING PHASE

Running

During this demonstration (which is considerably longer than a normal lesson) running practices are presented in five ways:

1 Running 'on the spot'.
2 Running about the hall (can be linked with other tasks at a signal).
3 Running round apparatus (e.g. rope, mat, block).
4 Running between and over apparatus.
5 Running, bounding, jumping and landing over apparatus.

Jumping and Landing

Free practice over or from a rope placed on the ground in the form of a circle—concentrating on:

1 Height and lightness of take-off and landing. (Quality.)
2 Different ways of jumping from the centre of the rope. (Variety.)
3 Variation in take-off (one or both feet). } (Increasing the degree
4 Twisting or turning in flight.   }   of limitation.)

Apparatus—Individual mats

Immediately the mats are placed and spaced out on the ground, the children practise their own individual sequences. Development has been on similar lines to those outlined in (*A*) (1–4). Here, however, the sequence is based not on an imposed task (Limitation Method), but on a combination of movements of the children's own choice (Indirect Method), i.e.

1 Practise one movement on your mat.
2 Practise different or other kinds of movements.
3 Now try to combine some of these movements.

187

4 Arrange these movements effectively into a sequence.
5 Can you add a new movement to your sequence?
6 Can you improve your sequence in some way?

BODY MOVEMENTS AND BALANCE (*combining tasks*)

1 Show different kinds of positions and practise different kinds of movements on your shoulders. (Plate 17.)
2 In your sequence try to include one or more positions of balance on your shoulders.

Part II

GROUP WORK

Details for the apparatus arrangement used in this lesson are illustrated in Fig. 23.

Lesson demonstrated by a class aged 10–11 years

Part I

THE INTRODUCTORY PHASE

1 *With apparatus*

In this phase the children have selected one (or more) of the undermentioned items of apparatus and practised with it for several lessons. They have been free (Indirect Method of presentation) to choose, devise and practise their own activities and movements, but the teacher, as in other phases of the lesson, has stimulated both quality and variety. In addition, the work has been developed through the principles of sequences and partner work. The latter includes one or more of the following ideas:

(*a*) The partner acting as an extra *obstacle* or item of apparatus.
(*b*) One child *assisting* another to help him/her to attempt and ultimately achieve activities or movements which otherwise he/she might never try and still less accomplish.
(*c*) One child *supporting* or *moving* a partner's *body weight*.
(*d*) *Matching* movements with a partner involving *unison* or *synchronised* work.

Items of apparatus from which a choice has been made:

Vaulting stool and box	Jumping boxes (height 12 in.,
Hoops, skittles and canes	24 in., 36 in.)
Poles and stands	Benches and trestles
Climbing frame	Large and small rubber mats

2 *Individual sequences, without apparatus* (Indirect Method of presentation). Children of Primary School age soon learn to appreciate the meaning of the term 'sequence'. For their benefit the teacher can make a parallel illustration with the word 'sentence', i.e. a combination of words; 'sequence' being a combination of movements.

Development in this particular lesson has been as follows:

(*a*) Combine two or more movements of your own choice.

(*b*) Think about the quality of the movements and also of their arrangement to make for smooth continuity.

(*c*) Can you extend your sequence or rearrange the movements within it to make it more effective?

(*d*) Now try to include a position of *balance*.

Now try to include a *bridging* or *arching* movement.

Now try to include a *rolling* or *twisting* movement.

Now try to include a *quick* and *slow* movement.

It will be seen that the conditions or tasks have been imposed progressively, making the children's work more interesting, challenging and demanding. This technique of imposing additional tasks can be used in almost every phase of the lesson, particularly in Group Work. For example: 'Can you, somewhere on your apparatus, use your *body upside down*?' or 'Use your body on your apparatus as *high* as you can', or 'Can you include a *balance* or a *twist* or a wide shape, etc., somewhere in your sequence?'

RUNNING, JUMPING AND LANDING

Running

In today's lesson the children base their practice on four factors:

1 Good use of space.	2 A good running style.
3 Variation of speed.	4 Variation of direction.

189

Earlier in their training each of these factors will have been taken separately and when a good standard has been obtained in one, e.g. the use of space, the teacher will have progressed to the next.

Jumping and Landing

1 Jumping and landing about the hall.
2 'Now try to show *wide shapes* in the air.' Once again the teacher will stimulate quality and variety. It must be appreciated that there are always many ways of solving the task.

Further development can be made by working (*a*) on sequences based on the task of wide shapes, but in ways other than jumping, and (*b*) on sequences initiated by a wide shape in the air and continued by adding the sequence practised in (*a*).

BALANCE

1 Find different ways of losing and regaining balance.
2 With a partner combine different 'matching' balance positions.

CLASS ACTIVITY—WORKING WITH PARTNERS

1 Free partner work with one child acting as the apparatus and the other moving over, off, or round the 'obstacle'.
2 Completely free partner work—for suggestions see notes on the Introductory Phase in this lesson—1.

Part II

GROUP WORK

Details of the apparatus for this lesson are illustrated in Fig. 41.

Group 1 The task is to devise and practise movements on different parts of the apparatus based on wide shapes (Plate 40).

Group 2 In this group the concentration is on direction and change of direction approaching and leaving the apparatus.

Group 3 The task is rolling round the pole with the emphasis on
(*a*) variation of shape;
(*b*) partner and group co-operation;

Group 4 No particular task has been imposed, but the group is stimulated to space themselves over the various parts of the apparatus, to be found working rather than

Primary school hall (42 ft × 29 ft)

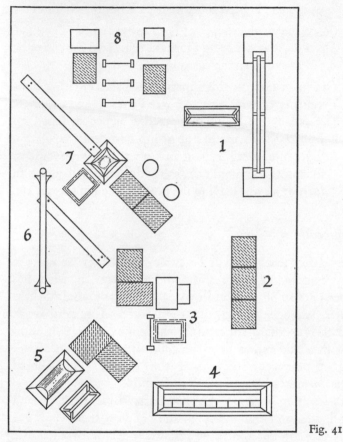

Fig. 41

group	apparatus	group	apparatus
1	Inverted bench on large jumping boxes (Plates 28), trestle.	6	Circular wooden pole on stands —3ft 3in. high (Plate 37), bench.
2	Three large rubber mats.	7	Inclined bench on vaulting stool, two large rubber mats, layered individual mats, two hoops.
3	One large, one small jumping box, two large rubber mats, cane on two skittles, layered individual mats.	8	One small, two large jumping boxes, two large rubber mats, three pairs of skittles supporting three canes.
4	Large climbing frame—7ft high (Plate 39).		
5	Vaulting box, two large rubber mats, trestle.		

See also Fig. 23 and the description of typical lessons in Chapter 10.

191

waiting and to use the equipment in as many different ways as possible.

Group 5 Jumping and rolling is the main task but the children try

(*a*) to match the shapes of both movements;

(*b*) to make contrasting shapes in these two movements;

(*c*) to move over the canes in different ways.

Group 6 The main task on this apparatus is balance, either individually or with a partner (see Plates 28 and 41).

Group 7 The task is to devise and practise sequences based on rolling—with partner or group co-operation.

Group 8 Although jumping, rolling and other agility movements constitute the main task, the additional challenge is to include a twist leaving the box, moving in the air, etc.

Final comments

We believe that teachers will be successful if they accept the principles involved, prepare thoroughly, reflect on what has already been accomplished, and make a critical appraisal of their own efforts. We believe, too, that the features of modern work are based on the sound educational philosophy that 'Education should fit the child rather than the child fitting the Education'. The current practice of describing this work as 'Educational Gymnastics' is not without some justification.

In every teaching situation, the facilities available, the approach or method used and the ability of the children themselves are important factors; but the most important factor of all is the teacher, whose help, guidance, stimulation and demands combine to do the best for each child.